Rethinking Panchayati Raj

Rethinking Panchayati Raj

Sanhita Joshi

Rawat Publications
Jaipur • New Delhi • Bangalore • Guwahati • Kolkata

ISBN 978-81-316-0851-7

Published by
Prem Rawat for **Rawat Publications**
Satyam Apts, Sector 3, Jawahar Nagar, Jaipur 302 004 (India)
Phone: 0141 265 1748 / 7006 Fax: 0141 265 1748
E-mail: info@rawatbooks.com
Website: www.rawatbooks.com

New Delhi Office
4858/24, Ansari Road, Daryaganj, New Delhi 110 002
Phone: 011 2326 3290

Also at *Bangalore, Guwahati* and *Kolkata*

Typeset by Rawat Computers, Jaipur
Printed at Chaman Enterprises, New Delhi

Contents

Acknowledgements

No work is really a product of a solitary scholar. While pursuing my research work, I came across many people who helped make this book a possibility and I wish to acknowledge them. At the outset, I would like to express my gratitude towards Lord Yogeshwar Krishna and Revered Pandurang Shastri Athavale.

I thank my PhD guide Dr B. Venkatesh Kumar for his guidance, help and motivation throughout my research journey. My PhD and consequently this book happened only because of his desire, way back in 2006, to make a presentation on the topic of 'Panchayati Raj and Contribution of Rajiv Gandhi' at the founding ceremony of the Rajiv Gandhi Centre for Contemporary Research, which was acclaimed for the freshness in its approach. After a couple of meetings with Venkatesh Sir, I decided to enter into full-fledged research and do a PhD, leaving behind my childhood dream of becoming an IAS officer. This twist in tale was the result of an honest realization that I probably was not suitable to be a bureaucrat and there lies an academician, a researcher and most importantly a teacher within me.

I must confess that I am a teacher's product. I cannot forget the extraordinary contribution of Professor Vikram Karandikar, who inspired and motivated me to develop a multidisciplinary orientation with a human touch. My teachers at Ruia College, Mumbai – Dr Vaibhavi Palsule, Dr Mrudul Nile – and above all my NCC guide Major Dr Rohini Shivbalan have played the most important role in developing me as a complete individual. I also extend my gratitude to all my postgraduate teachers and now my colleagues at the Department of Civics and Politics, University of Mumbai, for their support and motivation. I would like to specially thank Dr Sudha Mohan, head of the Department of Civics and Politics, University of Mumbai, for encouraging me to publish my work. I also would like to thank Dr Jose George for guiding me selflessly.

With great happiness I thank those anonymous referees whose reviews and comments helped me to refine and crystallize my work. Some parts of this book have been presented at national and international conferences. I am grateful to the learned audience who appreciated my work and also made important remarks. I want to particularly thank FLE Learning, Oxford (UK), and Rajiv Gandhi Centre for Contemporary Studies, University of Mumbai, for inviting me to present my work.

This book would not have been possible without the encouragement, endurance and support of my family. I am indebted to my father Shri Mahesh Joshi for whatever I have achieved in my life. I am a 'first-generation' postgraduate and PhD holder in my family. All this was only possible because of an open-minded father. His contribution in grooming my personality and instilling values in my life is beyond any expression. Thank you so much Papa! My mother Mrs Nirmala Joshi is the pillar of my life. Her kind and warm care has made me a complete human being. Very few in this world are blessed with good friends. I am proud of my family which also includes my sisters Pooja and Vinita with whom I could share anything and everything. It is a pleasure to thank my best friend Renuka Joshi for always being there for me.

Mr Rahul Joshi, my husband who is more of a friend, stood by me through thick and thin and encouraged me to write this book as initially I was a little reluctant to the idea. The book was taken up for serious writing after the birth of my two adorable kids Jayvart and Yashvrat. They helped me rediscover myself. I became adept at multitasking because of them. The maternity break gave that luxury and space to think freely and in the right direction. I would also like to thank my in-laws for supporting me always.

I express my deepest gratitude to all the Gram Sevaks, Block Development Officers, members of Gram Panchayats and villagers from Shahpur, Murbad and Kalyan-Dombivali talukas for cooperating and answering my queries. Academicians and scholars such as Girish Kumar, Niraja Gopal Jayal and Amit Prakash have extended a great help by giving their valuable comments. I gratefully acknowledge the financial support from the Narotam Sekhsaria Foundation while doing my research at the Rajiv Gandhi Centre for Contemporary Studies, University of Mumbai. I also thank the staff of Rajiv Gandhi Centre for Contemporary Studies and Department of Civics and Politics at the University of Mumbai.

Sanhita Joshi

1

Introduction

Globalization and decentralization are the twin ubiquitous ideas that have generated bewildering interest among people, academia, governments and policy makers during the last two decades. On one hand, globalization – through global commerce – is exacerbating income inequalities and trying to dictate terms on the developing nations, and on the other hand, it also gives immense opportunities to these developing countries especially for economic growth and development. It has opened new vistas for change through information and technological advancements. Yet another important phenomenon that is simultaneously taking shape across the globe is that many countries in the developed West and developing East representing different type of regimes are devolving powers to their units of local governance. It is done with the objective to achieve developmental goals in a swift and just manner. Concurrently, the idea of decentralization is also being promoted by international funding institutions, academicians and non-profit organizations. The reasons for promoting decentralization are multifarious. With the change in the philosophy of the state, objectives of the government, values and demands of the human kind, especially in a rapidly globalizing world, governance is being considered a significant agent of change, not only from above but also progressively more from below. The conflict today is seen between the archaic forms of public governance manifested in the form of bureaucratic administration or commandist administration (Manor, 1999) and the modern-day forms of democratic, flexible, efficient, transparent and decentralized governance. Values such as efficiency and economy today have gained quintessential momentum. Osborne and Gaibler's book *Reinventing Government* published in 1992 explains this critical importance of decentralized governance in the context of a market-oriented ecology well.

The idea of governance has undergone a complete overhaul because of rising public awareness, mounting people's expectations, information technology (IT) revolution, better connectivity and rapid integration of the world owing to globalizing economies. Efficiency, economy, accountability and responsibility are the paradigm indices to evaluate the performance of institutions of governance. The discourse on development also entails that governments must shed a 'commandist' and centralized approach and adopt a more democratic and decentralized disposition. It is argued that efficient decision-making can be facilitated by decentralization and delegation of power. Decentralization has been looked at as a singularly useful mode of governance to deliver the public services from convenient local centres close to the client's locality. Bringing governance to the doorstep of the citizens and forging a direct relationship between the client and the government have been the driving force behind the process of decentralization worldwide. Decentralization is expected to release local energies and enlist local support for carrying out development-oriented activities. The spread of democracy, especially after the

World War II, has created a sturdy foundation for decentralization. It is said that 'democracy is fundamentally a decentralized system'. A centralized administration however efficient it may be can never excel the basic idea of democracy, that is, government by the people (Dubey and Padalia, 2002).

Theoretical Framework

India suffered the massive economic crisis in early 1990s, which eventually compelled her to embark upon the path of liberalization, privatization and globalization. The 'New Economic Policy' was introduced in India in 1991, which significantly transformed the Indian economy. It was obvious to deduce that it will have some impact on the polity as well. It is fascinating to note that in the following year two historic constitutional amendments were passed by the Indian parliament. The 73rd and 74th Constitutional Amendments formally created the third tier of governance. Its significance lies in the fact that the amendments gave local bodies a constitutional status, at both urban and rural levels. In a way, globalization and decentralization happened simultaneously in India. Therefore, it is very important to study these two events together and examine whether one has any impact on the other or not. There was a fear looming large that as the state shrinks in size and withdraws itself from various social sector responsibilities, problems and concerns of the people will increasingly go unheard and will be poorly represented. However, studies have indicated that the role of state does not diminish with globalization, rather its criticality increases (Sathe, 2009). The World Commission on Social Dimension of Globalization (2006) recognizes the opportunities for a better life that globalization presents. It is believed that people's hopes are realizable, but only if globalization is subjected to better governance at all levels. The whole discourse on development and governance encapsulates the significance of decentralization today.

The present book purports to examine the functioning of the local self-governing institutions in India in the backdrop of changes that globalization has introduced to village polity though not directly but indirectly. The major interest of this book is in understanding the practice of local governance, that is, Panchayati Raj Institutions (PRIs), especially after these institutions got a constitutional status. Also, it is interesting to study them in the backdrop of globalization that occurred in India almost during the same time. Some of the significant questions that the author wanted to look at are as follows:

1. Do globalization and the changes brought along with it provide an opportunity to people at the grassroots to empower their position, and deal with their developmental and socio-economic problems on their own?
2. What is the status of public services at the grassroots in the context of globalization and how local institutions are dealing with it?
3. Does greater flow of information and access to technology improve the conditions at the local level?

The world is fast becoming a place without borders. Borders of ideas, civilizations, cultures and economies are being eroded. The geo-political borders are also only to maintain fast diminishing national identities in an integrated world. There has been a progressive international economic integration of the world since 1950s. A phenomenal growth has been reported in international trade, investment and finance. This has led to a greater economic openness resulting in free flow of not only trade, investment and finance but also service, technology, information and ideas across national boundaries (Nayyar, 2002). Shrinking distances are forcing us to think about the world as a unit, which may lead to nurturing a tendency to homogenize. Many critics of globalization argue that globalization is another form of international capitalism. However, the current wave of globalization offers each one a chance, an opportunity to dominate the international market due to the kind of openness it provides.[1] Nonetheless, it cannot be disputed that it has led to uneven development. Hegemonic circles are created in different parts of the world, creating an environment of 'loss of choice' at the regional, domestic and local levels. Transnational companies are playing 'intrusive politics'.[2] This has further led to the 'problem of exclusion'. Fruits of development are being cornered by selected few and not going unto the last. Therefore, it becomes necessary responsibility to interfere on the part of the government. Welfare politics targets to achieve symmetrical development in which government is responsible to provide and cater to the needs of the people. For this, they are also held responsible at regular intervals through elections. But, in a globalized world, this responsibility is difficult to be demanded. This actually is accentuating the process of exclusion.

In this context, the role of the state (government) becomes even more important in spite of the fact that globalization is intruding into the political periphery of the state. Many argue that globalization is rendering the Westphalia model of the state obsolete. However, looking at this from a different perspective, it also suggests a transition in the entire role, range and reach of the state. The failure of the centralized state, in both economic and political governance, has swung the pendulum in favour of decentralized system across the globe in recent years (Rao Govinda, 2005).

An immediate effect of globalization has been the impact of the world capital market on centralized and decentralized governance especially with respect to making vital decisions that affect the lives of the people (Kothari, 1989). Globalization also creates legitimacy vacuum. As globalization encroaches upon a nation-state's economic sovereignty, it is compelled to create local democratic structures to further its political sovereignty and retain its legitimacy (Tremblay, 2001). Today for a state with multiple level governments, the process of decentralization, which is the transfer of authority or responsibility to local governments, is often seen as an important condition for economic development. Decentralization is a countervailing trend to globalization, which ensures that growth process is pro-poor, pro-women, pro-nature and pro-jobs. In a sense, as Ash (1994) states, there is double movement of globalization on one hand and devolution, decentralization and localization on the other hand, which has been termed as *glocalization*. 'Globalization is like a giant wave that can either capsize nations or carry them forward. Successful localization creates a situation where local entities and other groups in society "the crew of the boat if you will" are free to exercise individual autonomy but also have incentives to work together'.[3]

Globalization has created complexities of social, economic and even political in nature. When we think about a globalized world, every nation is a unit of this entity and has to fight these complexities and find answers to erupting questions of modern polities. The self-regarding actions of an individual makes him or her think about only profit maximization, which is the goal of everyone in this materialist world be it an individual, a family, a society, a state or world at large. So, there are conflicting interests in today's pluralist societies, which creates many challenges to be faced especially by the governments that have to find solutions to these challenges. Furthermore, in this globalized and competitive world, today, individual is at the centre of discussion. It is important to develop their capacities to fight and counter the challenges. The role of any government would be to enhance capability sets (Sen, 2000) of citizens being governed. This leads to enhancements of their personal security and freedom to make choices. Therefore, there is a need to identify a fundamental shift in the purpose and methods of government (George, 2008).

Globalization, in its primary sense, means expansion of economic transactions and the organization of economic activities across the political boundaries of nation-states. So it is pertaining not only to market economy but also to political democracy (Nayyar, 2002). Globalization usually implies increase in trade, investment, technology and labour flows between economies. It was expected by some that as globalization occurs, the state would wither away. 'Many participants in the globalization debate seem to agree about the decreasing economic, political, and cultural importance of (nation-) state. From above the central role of state is being hollowed out by international political organization and below by the growing phenomenon of local government, which seems to have become the example of what good governance should be about' (Schuurman, 2001: 8). Similarly, Lieten (2003: 26) has argued that 'the agenda of decentralization fits another agenda, namely, the agenda of globalization and the rolling back of the state. Globalization actually sucks the local into centralizing process of the free market. Nation-States are somewhat receding and ceding sovereign power to market forces'. Palanithurai and Ramesh (2008) states that people, especially marginalized sections of the society at the grassroots level will bear the brunt of globalization the most. It has to be to be mitigated through micro actions in the field and macro actions through policies and decisions. (Palanithurai and Ramesh, 2008). It is generally accepted that the state has a very crucial role to play in the provision of basic public services especially to the marginalized sections as they cannot access market for these services. In a village in India, it is the responsibility of the locally elected body, that is, the Gram Panchayat, to provide these basic public services. While decentralization has undoubtedly gained popularity within the last two decades, it is not a new concept. The term *decentralization* attracted attention in the 1950s and 1960s when British and French colonial administrations prepared colonies for independence by devolving responsibilities for certain programmes to local authorities. In the 1980s, decentralization came to the forefront of the development agenda alongside the renewed global emphasis on governance and human-centred approaches to human development. Today, both developed and developing countries are pursing decentralization policies.

There is a worldwide research now going on especially in the developing countries to craft institutions and administrative processes that would successfully deliver developmental goals with people's own active engagement, ensuring authenticity, inclusiveness, transparency and social justice. *The World Development Report* focused on the globalization and localization and saw localization as revitalizing the local realm by raising levels of participation and involvement and providing people with a greater ability to shape their own lives. *The World Development Report* (1999) recognizes the importance of the local for raising levels of participation and providing people with greater ability to shape the context of their lives. It is here that the vertical structure of power get decentralized, horizontalized and democratized and is rooted locally in the political, social and economic organizations of the people and themselves. Any democratic polity in order to ensure good governance should provide citizens with what Habermas describes as the public sphere. With Habitat II or the City Summit in 1996, the General Assembly of the United Nations officially recognized the vitality of local politics and importance of local variations in the era of globalization. Globalization is rendering the public sphere competitive and people need to be provided with an enabling environment to fight inequalities created by it.

Globalization is also identified as one of the reasons for the growth in the era of local governance. It is also called The Age of Local Governance (Denters and Lawrence, 2005). According to Denters and Lawrence (2005), following trends have led to decentralization. However, their study is primarily focused upon European and Western countries. But some of the factors do have resonance for developing nations as well:

Micro Trends

1. Modernization of individual citizen.
2. Citizen orientation towards governments has changed. Government's legitimacy is dependent on its performance.
3. Increase in skills of the citizens due to the rise of new channels of participation, increased education.

Macro Trends

1. Urbanization, globalization (social exclusion and environmental concerns)
2. (i) European integration

   (ii) Funds for local governments

   (iii) Changed balance of power

The entire literature available on this topic today focuses on the nexus between globalization and local governance or decentralization. Various models and methods are being developed to counter the problems posed by globalization. Local governance units are also seen as one of the panacea to this phenomenon. In this context, panchayats as people's institutions of self-governance have a critical role to play. One of the ill-effects of globalization is believed to be erosion or dilution of the state authority. In the process the state is devoid of its legitimacy or at least it becomes vulnerable. In the opinion of many scholars decentralization of powers and authority towards the grassroots units is considered as a positive step to maintain this diminishing legitimacy (Palanithurai and Ramesh, 2008). The idea of an Indian rural area or a village is also changing fast. It is in a state of flux. However, one cannot eliminate the discourses on the caste and gender while looking at politics taking shape in rural India. The Indian government immediately after independence embarked on the project of rural development. The central government created its own administrative hierarchy for rural development with plethora of special programmes that all bypassed the so-called PRIs. In the next six decades after independence, India remained committed to strengthening the roots of decentralized governance. Many committees and commissions were appointed, which have made recommendations that crystallize its role and functions in the present set-up. Nevertheless, the mere decentralization of powers is meaningless and an empty idea in the absence of a literate, aware, informed and skilled citizenry, for they are the true bearers of power. This also needs be contextualized in the fast globalizing India to understand impact of both on each other. Those who are at helms of affairs at the grassroots are to be trained in the craft of governance to deal with changes introduced by globalization. Leaders at grassroots level who manage the local affairs have to be made aware of the implications of globalization and hence they have to be sensitized (Palanithurai and Ramesh, 2008). Today, the idea of decentralization is associated with 'good governance' (Lieten, 2003: 17). There was increasing feeling that 'these people, however poor and illiterate, however much repressed by gender, caste and class, have a richness of thought that needs to be tapped much more than has been done so far' (Lieten, 2003: 13). Why India is an important case of study is the fact that it has been able to create a wide democratic base today. The expansion of the PRIs in their new form is a very significant movement as, earlier, Lok Sabha, Rajya Sabha and 25 State Assemblies and two union territories (UTs) used to elect only 4,963 members. Today, every five years, 30 lakh (i.e. 3 million) representatives are elected out of which 10 lakh (i.e. 33%) are women and 22.5 per cent seats belong to Scheduled Castes (SCs) and Scheduled Tribes (STs) (Institute of Social Sciences, 2000: 10).

PRIs as Central Processing Units of Democracy

The present anthology tries to visualize PRIs as the central processing units (CPU) of Indian democracy. It attempts to look at the practice of Panchayati Raj and selectively avoids a detailed institutional discussion. These grassroots level units are the schools of our democracy. If they are fed with appropriate inputs, then it will be easier to earn outputs that will strengthen democracy as whole in our country. Hence, while focusing on the PRIs in India, the book has meticulously tried to look at issues of empowerment of people, delivery and availability of public services, issues pertaining to capacity building (social capital)[4] and social audit. It is well recognized that local bodies have an important role to play in the democratic process and in meeting the basic requirements of the people. The old adage, 'for every citizen, most government is local government', still holds good. However, the ground analysis of PRIs reveals that they have not been honestly vested with the powers, functions and financial resources and necessary autonomy. In fact, it still remains a rubber stamp third tier of Indian federalism (Tremblay, 2001). Financial paucity is the biggest problem faced by the PRIs. And, if PRIs are to work as prime mechanism of development, then they have to be given proper financial aid, especially in a global world.

Defining the Topic

The concept of 'governance' is quite clearly broader than that of 'government' alone. 'Governance' has been defined by the World Bank as the traditions and institutions by which authority is exercised for the common good (The World Bank, 1992). Along with the institutions, effective governance also tries to develop the 'voice' of the people, which they need in order to improve the accountability and efficiency of the government (Harriss, 2007).

Globalization is a complex and multidimensional process. However, the study shall confine itself to the meaning of globalization as greater connectivity, greater access, greater knowledge and good technology. Global challenges are varied right from environment protection to sustainable development to empowering the marginalized people at the base of a democracy. The book also prefers to stick to deal with empowering people at the grassroots amidst global forces.

'Governance' is broadly defined as the system of values, policies and institutions by which a society organizes collective decision-making and action related to political, economic and socio-cultural and environmental affairs through the interaction of the state, civil society and the private sector. Governance comprises the complex mechanisms, processes and institutions through which citizens and groups articulate their interests, mediate their differences and exercise their legal rights and obligations.

Local governments throughout the world (Western industrialized world) played a major role in the delivery of fundamental collective public and quasi-public goods. Local governments have begun to develop a leadership role in some of the broader challenges of community government, especially in the current context of globalization. The present century has to fight many global challenges with local initiatives and local efforts. Some of the common global challenges are poverty, hunger, elementary education and empowerment of the weaker sections of the society as Marx called them the 'have-nots'.

In the present study, governance has been defined not only as the availability of basic public services to the marginalized sections in a village but also as enlarged participation of the people in the developmental activities. The study also tried to consider the quality and quantity of devolution of powers at the grassroots and how far the Gram Panchayats have been using it for their own benefits. It believes that it is the responsibility of the state to provide these services and in a village the responsibility would fall on the local self-government, that is, the Gram Panchayats.

Research Methodology

In order to collect first-hand information (i.e. primary data), the participant observation method was used. A ground-level field survey of shortlisted villages was conducted using ethnographic method. The research team personally visited each Gram Panchayat and spoke to different actors involved in the process of local governance practice such as the Gram Sevak, Sarpanch and people of the villages. During the visits, the working conditions of the Gram Panchayats, responses given by the people and availability of basic services at the grassroots were observed. The micro analysis of accumulated qualitative information gave some important insights. A comparative analysis of the quality and availability of the basic public services provided by the PRIs at the grassroots, extent of participation of people in general and women in specific and style of functioning of the PRIs was done using the descriptive statistics such as frequencies, mean and percentage. The language of communication with local people as well as all office bearers at the grassroots was Marathi. The knowledge of local language helped a lot to reach out to people and talk to them with extreme ease. A close-ended questionnaire was originally prepared in Marathi and was circulated among randomly picked up villagers. Nonetheless it was very obvious that such microscopic study of few villages cannot lead us to a generalization that holds true for the entire country. There is no claim made here that this study helps to understand the general phenomena or the contemporary state of affairs in village politics. But this work definitely generates some useful insights into the practice of local governance in Thane district, which was a rather less researched area so far. It validates the existing analytical frameworks and also tries to add to it by studying routine practice of Panchayati Raj in these villages.

Selection of Sample Villages

The state of Maharashtra was selected because it has a better record with respect to the PRIs than the other states. The choice of Thane district was a much deliberate choice for a simple reason that it is one of the most urbanized districts in the state of Maharashtra. This was also a district where global forces have played a dominant role in bringing changes in not only people's economic life but also social and political life. In this district, there are a total of 15 talukas, out of which Shahpur, Murbad and Kalyan talukas were shortlisted for study. It was very difficult to choose Gram Panchayats from these talukas as there are a total of 228 villages in Shahpur, 206 in Murbad and 69 in Kalyan taluka. Keeping in mind the variety in the socio-economic and inter- and intra-regional differences, it was not advisable to make a big sample size. The objective of the study was to search for more qualitative facts than quantitative facts. Therefore, within the given resources, time frame and scale on which this research was designed, it was decided to stick to a small and manageable sample size to collect primary data. The facts collected from the field were substantiated by the works and findings of the previous scholars. Accordingly, two villages from each taluka were picked up after consulting the Block Development Officer (BDO) of the concerned taluka. These were Azade Gaon and Katai from Kalyan taluka, Khandpe and Ambele Budruk from Murbad taluka and Gotheghar, Kalbhunde and Wafe from Shahpur taluka. Kalbhunde village from Shahpur taluka was only visited once because of difficulty in reaching the village.

Besides, important officials from various units of local governance, for example, BDOs of Shahpur, Murbad and Kalyan talukas, Gram Sevaks of seven villages visited and members of panchayats were interacted. The primary data collection also included information through semi-structured interviews of scholars and experts on the subject. These included Dr Niraja Gopal Jayal, Dr Amit Prakash from Jawaharlal Nehru University and Girish Kumar from Indian Institute of Public Administration, New Delhi.

Limitations of the Research

The journey to explore the various dimensions related to the subject was not free from limitations. In order to understand and grasp the details of the theme, the study used specific meanings of terms used in this research subjects.

Accordingly, the multifaceted terms such as local governance and globalization were analysed and used considering one of their contextual meanings. It was difficult and too lengthy to include all its definitional aspects. Another limitation was related to the basic nature of the terms studied. It was difficult not only to specifically define the terms but also to find an apt set of samples because the terms such as local governance in the context of globalization are less quantitative and more qualitative variables in nature. After talking to the BDOs of various talukas and using their suggestions, two villages each were shortlisted per taluka randomly to gather ground reality and first-hand information, which was then analysed both qualitatively and quantitatively. Before generalizing the recommendations to all states or villages uniformly, care should be taken to study laws of the concerned states, their socio-economic background, presence and hold of various political parties, elite capture, caste compositions and historical developments. The major limitation of the research was a small sample size owing to time constraint, and therefore it was not representative of India. There are many inter- and intra-regional differences within the state so it was difficult to consider all variables through a large but unmanageable sample size. Therefore, an extended research including the facts from other states of India is recommended for more reliable findings.

Scheme of Chapterization

The second chapter explores the idea of local governance and decentralization and various dimensions attached to it and try to place it in context of globalization and global challenges. This chapter takes a comprehensive overview of emergence of decentralization and local governance by examining the reasons for it and also putting in place various types and modes of decentralization. It quests to answer questions such as whether local governance could be seen as a panacea to issues and problems encountered at the local level in this globalized world. This chapter also tries to explore the idea of good governance, for it is today increasingly considered as a function of local governance.

The third chapter introduces the reader to the historical moorings and evolution of the concept of PRIs in India. It takes the reader for a ride into the ancient period and traces its development during the British period to till date. It also focuses on the efforts of various governments and the commissions that the Government of India appointed in making PRIs a reality.

The system of local governance in the state of Maharashtra has been dealt with at length in fourth chapter.

The fifth chapter discusses in details the findings of the field work conducted in Thane district from the state of Maharashtra. The chapter covers a host of important issues including electoral process and practices, functioning of Gram Sabha, people's empowerment and deepening of democratic values through the assessment of selected villages and interrogating them with the original objectives of the decentralization. It examines the ground realities of the PRIs from the Thane district of the state of Maharashtra. It evaluates its efficacy and efficiency in the light of whether the objectives laid down in the 73rd Constitutional Amendment Act have been realized or not. Throughout the chapter an attempt is made to deepen the understanding of the importance of local governance as a medium to advance humanitarian values, percolation of equality and building a strong community life.

The sixth chapter is dedicated to the functioning of PRIs in India and tries to analyse their role in the context of the globalization and global challenges. It is the time to redefine and revitalize their role in the present scenario. The chapter attempts to deduce that PRIs are the CPU of the democracy. The chapter reports from its field study successful implementation of a World Bank-funded project for piped water supply in a bunch of villages from the Shahpur block of Thane district. This particular scheme has changed the lives of people at the grassroots; it aided people in instilling values of equality and community control of common property resource and fast disappearing resource such as water. It also makes a comparative analysis of Panchayati Raj system and its practice in Maharashtra with other states such as Madhya Pradesh, Karnataka, West Bengal and Kerala. This chapter also discusses few recommendations on some poignant issues plaguing the local level politics. It neither tries to romanticize the idea of decentralization nor does it overlook its successful implementation in various countries as well as in some states of India.

Notes

1. Recently, ex-US Foreign Secretary of State Henry Kissinger said that the centre of gravity is shifted to now Asia (China).
2. *Talk on Globalization: A Critical Perspective* by Professor Rajen G. Harshe, eminent political scientist and Vice Chancellor, University of Allahabad on 18 December 2007, at University of Mumbai.
3. Joseph Stiglitz, former World Bank Chief Economist and Senior Vice-President for Development Economics.
4. This concept has been mooted by James Coleman and further developed by Robert Putnam.

2

Decoding Decentralization, Local Governance and Good Governance

The prime focus of the present chapter is to look at the idea of decentralization, local governance and good governance from multiple perspectives. It aims at bringing these ideas together to assess their feasibility in globalization context. All over the world the trend towards decentralization or devolution of powers, functions and functionaries at the local level has been in vogue since the late 1970s. The language of governance – popularized by the World Bank, which also is a major part of its reform advocacy – has forced developing and transition economies to adopt the decentralized way of functioning. Furthermore, in response to the challenges posed by greater globalization and consequent integration of the world through market economy, more and more developed as well as developing countries are now devolving powers to the lower units of government. However, the causes and reasons behind the process of decentralization have been myriad and differ from country to country. The term *decentralization* attracted attention in the 1950s and 1960s when British and French colonial administrations prepared colonies for independence by devolving responsibilities for certain programmes to local authorities. In 1980s, decentralization came to the forefront of the development agenda alongside the renewed global emphasis on governance and human-centred approaches to human development (UNDP, 2002).[1] In the early 20th century, centralization and commandist governance had helped many regions to cope with the consequences of the great depression and adverse effects on polity and economy of the World War I and especially World War II (Manor, 1999).[2] Command economy, planning and state funding, all these led many countries, especially newly independent countries, to the path of fast economic growth and development. There was a consequent unprecedented expansion in the public services and welfare state provisions in Western Europe and North America. However, soon, these centralized systems found themselves trapped in the web of undermined capacity, huge burden of public expenditure and a leviathan government. Confidence in centralized approaches to the management of national economies was shaken in the late 1960s and 1970s. This defining change in the way the state was perceived paved way for greater decentralization for better governance. The growing economic crisis of 1970s was compounded by political failures in the less developed countries of Asia, Africa and Latin America. The euphoric socialist experiment of Soviet Russia was vehemently criticized and it crumbled under the weight of its own over-centralized state capitalist system. The biggest challenge before such system was procuring and sustaining legitimacy. Legitimacy of such autocratic or one-party rule or commandist rulers was challenged in the absence of low or no economic growth (designed by following the Keynesian or Leninist approaches to economies). These factors created a favourable environment to nurture the faith in the ideals of democracy especially grassroots democracy by the way of decentralization.

The period of 1990s brought totally a new age of hope and aspirations clubbed with power of knowledge and information technology. The frontiers of nations were getting eroded through greater integration of the world by the way of liberalization, privatization and globalization. Thus, a demand for reorienting the role, range and reach of the government came to the forefront. Along with privatization and deregulation, this shift represents a substantial reduction in the authority of national governments over economic policy (Bardhan and Mukherjee, 2007).[3] As Mohan (2005: 2)[4] also suggests, 'Globalization, the other important development, was threatening to make the governments too big and too small. It was too big for small things occurring at the urban/rural local level and too small for problems emerging at the global level. These fundamental changes challenged the role of the government, compelling it to redefine and reorient its role and relevance'. There were efforts being made to search for new paradigms of development under the pressures of emerging ideas such as sustainable development, equitable growth, inclusive development and people's participation.

Motivation Behind Decentralization

Globalization has brought profuse changes in the economic activities of countries and has also caused corresponding alterations in the political and social settings. The contours of the governance system are also changing so as to adapt to the approaching challenges of the 21st century at all levels. The Millennium Development Goals (MDGs)[5] which were set to be achieved by 2015 also testify to the fact that countries are now gearing up to reshape their governance to achieve the target before the deadline. First, decentralization is necessary to accelerate the pace of growth and development and also spread the benefits of growth equitably, integrate diverse regions and use scarce resources more efficiently to promote development in poverty-stricken or economically backward areas. Second, poorest groups are to obtain a larger share of government services and means must be found to decentralize public service delivery and involve the beneficiaries in planning and decision-making at all levels and particularly at the local level.

The motivation for the decentralization has been varied. In Eastern Europe and the former Soviet Union, it was part of the political and economic transformation; in Latin America, it was to reinforce the transition to democracy; in South Africa, Sri Lanka and Indonesia, it was a response to ethnic or regional conflict; and in Chile, Uganda and Cote d'Ivoire, it was to improve the delivery of basic services (Shah and Shah, 2006). When we overview decentralization in India, we find that almost all the above-mentioned concerns have in one or the other way influenced and shaped the journey of decentralized democracy through panchayats. Gupta (2004) has very convincingly analysed and tried to generalize the reasons of decentralization worldwide[6]:

1. Degeneration of patronage system.
2. Over-centralization leading to undermining autonomy, ineffective and non-responsive governance and increasing corruption.
3. Colonial masters giving the way out.
4. Industrial development in a decentralized way.
5. Donor agencies around 1980s sought the participation of micro actors at the grassroots in the developmental programmes.
6. Failure of centralized system in East Europe.
7. Spread of democracy.
8. Cultural and traditional environment.

Meaning of Decentralization

Theoretically decentralization is basically a framework to share and devolve powers, functions and responsibilities between different tiers of a government. It ensures efficiency, democratic participation and enhances annals of peoples' voices and choices. According to Aldous Huxley, 'the political road to a better society is the road of decentralization and responsible self-government'. Decentralization is typically viewed as an important element of participatory democracy that allows citizens to have an opportunity to communicate their preferences and views to elected officials who are subsequently rendered accountable for their performance to citizens (Bardhan and Mukherjee, 2007).[7] Bardhan and Mukherjee (2007) also present a list of prerequisites for effective decentralization and a local democracy:

1. Educated and politically aware citizenry.
2. Absence of high inequality in economic or social status that inhibits political participation of the poor or of the minorities.
3. Prevalence of law and order.
4. Conduct of free and fair elections according to the constitutional setting that prevents excessive advantage to incumbents.
5. Effective competition between political candidates or parties with long-term interests.
6. Presence of reliable channels of information to citizens.
7. Presence of oversight mechanisms.

Decentralization is a complex phenomenon involving many geographic entities, societal actors and social sectors. The geographic entities include the international, national, subnational and local. The societal actors include government, the private sector and civil society. The social sectors include all development themes – political, social, cultural and environmental.[8]

A Mix of Four Dimensions

Decentralization involves four dimensions: the collective/exterior, the collective/interior, the individual/ exterior and the individual/interior.[9]

1. The *collective/exterior* has to do with the institutional and legal forms and procedures.
2. The *collective/interior* deals with the societal culture – the set of values and assumptions, which are often unspoken or unacknowledged but nevertheless play a powerful role in human relationships.
3. The *individual/exterior* dimension has to do with the observable behaviour of individuals within the various societal institutions, whether government, private sector or civil society.
4. The dimension of the *individual/interior* deals with the mindset, world view, mental models, emotions and intuitions of individuals within institutions.

Types of Decentralization

Decentralization is complex process and encompasses a wide range of elements (Manor, 1999).[10] There are three broad types of decentralization, namely, political, administrative and fiscal, and four major forms of decentralization, namely, devolution, delegation, deconcentration and disinvestment.

Political Decentralization

Appropriate powers and authorities are devolved to the elected units of the government at the lowest tier of the government so that they are enabled to expedite local service delivery and invite participation. Devolution is a type of political decentralization. Political decentralization is generally and ideally ensured through a constitutional mandate.

Fiscal Decentralization

Resource allocation in the form of taxation powers to the subnational tiers of government or provision of grants is the crux of financial decentralization. This type is an important requisite for the capacity building of Local Government Units as their successful functioning largely depends on their good financial health.

Administrative Decentralization

Administrative decentralization aims at transferring decision-making authority, resources and responsibilities for the delivery of select number of public services from the central government to other levels of government, agencies, and field offices of central government line agencies (UNDP, 2002).[11] This type of decentralization generally involves two forms, namely, deconcentration and delegation.

Objectives of Decentralization

Decentralization is merely a medium to achieve the larger goal of well-rounded human development, which is sustainable as well. Today, worldwide, countries have recognized the importance of decentralized democratic forms of government as they serve multiple objectives:

1. Creates responsible and responsive local government.
2. Open government.
3. Representative government.
4. Efficient and effective government.
5. Government that encourages community participation.

6. Better prioritization of needs.
7. Better service delivery.
8. Easy to address issues of gender equity, empowerment of marginalized and environment protection and regeneration.
9. Offloading the central government.
10. Control at points of service delivery and improving effectiveness and accountability.
11. A matching local structures under local circumstances.
12. Greater financial accountability.
13. Deepening of democracy.

Guiding Principles of Reframing Governance

In the rapidly changing globe and global actors and the role of the state as a whole, it has become necessary to reframe the public bodies, especially the one which caters to the needs of the people. These bodies clothed with legitimacy prove to be more responsible and responsive to the needs and problems of the people who are their masters. From the governance point of view, it has today become necessary to redraw the lower tiers of government and necessary powers and functions endowed upon them to handle things with a local touch. Therefore, we need to look at the principles that can be taken into consideration to craft the governance system in the changed scenario.

Principle of Subsidiarity

The principle of subsidiarity stipulates that functions shall be carried out closest to citizens at the smallest unit of governance possible and delegated upwards only when the local unit cannot perform the task. In this scheme, the citizen and the community are the centre of governance. In place of traditional hierarchies, there will be ever-enlarging concentric circles of government and delegation is outward depending on necessity (ARC, 2006).[12] According to this principle, taxing, spending and regulatory functions should be exercised by lower levels of government unless a convincing case can be made for assigning them to higher levels of government. This principle evolved from the social teaching of the Roman Catholic Church and was first proposed by Pope Leo XIII in 1891. Subsequently, Pope Pius XI highlighted the principle of subsidiarity as a third way between dictatorship and a laissez-faire approach to governance (Shah and Shah, 2006).[13]

Democratic Decentralization

While subsidiarity should be the overarching principle in restructuring governance, in practical constitutional terms it can be applied only through effective decentralization. The decentralization theorem advanced by Oates states that 'each public service should be provided by the jurisdiction having control over the minimum geographic area that would internalize benefits and costs of such provision'.[14] In the ultimate analysis, all governance processes are about fulfilling the citizens' aspirations and needs. Decentralization is a potent tool to counter the phenomenal asymmetry in the locus of power and the imbalance in the exercise of power (ARC, 2006).[15]

Clear Delineation of Functions

In a federal democracy, the roles and responsibilities of various tiers of government have to be clearly defined. This leads to clarity in terms of functional areas and concerned powers and authorities. The jurisdictional design should be so specific that it will allow the player, that is, the units of governance to prepare their work plan. This also avoids duplication of work and saves time, money and energy to a great extent.

Real Devolution of Powers

The principles of subsidiarity and democratic decentralization cannot be operationalized by mere creation of elaborate structures and periodic elections. Devolution, to be real and meaningful, demands that local governments should be effectively empowered to frame regulations, take decisions and enforce their will within their legitimate sphere of action. Such empowerment should be clearly and unambiguously defined by the Constitution and state legislatures.

Meaning of Local Governance

Local governments are the lower level units of administration and governance. They are formally created and endowed with specific powers and functions and sometimes equivalent financial support too. They represent the legitimate wing of the government at the centre. It epitomizes the idea of direct democracy at the lowest tier of governance hierarchy. In the opinion of Shah and Shah (2006),[16] local government refers to specific institutions or entities created by:

1. national constitutions (Brazil, Denmark, France, India, Italy, Japan and Sweden)
2. by state constitutions (Australia and the United States)
3. by ordinary legislation of a higher level of central government (New Zealand, the United Kingdom and most countries)
4. by provincial or state legislation (Canada and Pakistan)
5. or by executive order (China) to deliver a range of specified services to a relatively small geographically delineated area.

Local Governance: A Broader Concept

Local governance is a broader concept and is defined as the formulation and execution of collective action at the local level. Thus, it encompasses the direct and indirect roles of formal institutions of local government and government hierarchies, as well as the roles of informal norms, networks, community organizations, and neighbourhood associations in pursuing collective action by defining the framework for citizen–citizen and citizen–state interactions, collective decision-making and delivery of local public services (Shah and Shah, 2006).[17] Local governance, therefore, includes the diverse objectives of vibrant, living, working and environmentally preserved self-governing communities. Good local governance is not just about providing a range of local services but also about preserving the life and liberty of residents, creating space for democratic participation and civic dialogue, and environmentally sustainable local development, and facilitating outcomes that enrich the quality of life of residents.

Although the concept of local governance is as old as the history of humanity, only recently has it entered the broad discourse in the academic and practice literature. Globalization and the information revolution are forcing a re-examination of citizen–state relations and roles and the relationships of various orders of government with entities beyond government and thereby an enhanced focus on local governance. Local governments throughout the Western industrialized world played a major role in the delivery of fundamental collective public and quasi-public goods. Local governments have begun to develop a leadership role in some of the broader challenges of community governance. The concept of governance is also changing. Governance should enhance the capability sets of the people being governed, leading to enhancement in their personal security, freedom to make choices and welfare as measured by such indices as the United Nations Human Development Index. Governance would also include public decision-making concerning local issues, increasingly involves multi-agency working partnerships and policy networks which cut across organizational boundaries. Local governance that is responsive (doing the right thing – delivering services that are consistent with citizens' preferences or are citizen focused); responsible (doing the right thing the right way – working better but costing less and benchmarking with the best) and accountable (to citizens, through a rights-based approach).

The Indian Scenario

India has been one of the forerunners in the development and strengthening of local governance through decentralization. In the Indian context, economic reforms and Panchayati Raj have been the two major policy imperatives since the early 1990s (UNDP, 2000).[18] The seeds of village governance were sown early in the pre-independence period during the freedom struggle itself. India is a home to the concept of village democracy because since Vedic period this motherland had the system of village governance in the form of Gram Panchayats.[19] The resolution of the Indian National Congress in 1947 reads like this: 'The smallest territorial unit should be able to exercise effective control over its corporate life by means of a popularly elected panchayat'. After independence, the Directive Principles of State Policy under Article 40 in Part VI of the Constitution were largely ignored for four decades (1950–1990) – a period where 'centralization' was the dominant principle of governance.

The process of centralized governance was underpinned by an ideology of planned development (centralized allocation of resources by the Planning Commission; a state-led programme for investments in industry and infrastructure; the belief that the state should control and direct the commanding heights of the economy) and a bureaucratic system of controls and regulation, inherited from a colonial government.[20]

India's development agenda, which is heavily depended on state finance and conveniently ignored the competitive element that market brings with it, was one of the causes of our inability to address the problem of poverty and unequal growth. The impulse for decentralization (from the late 1980s in the case of the central government) is also traced to the recognition of the failure of centralized mode of decision-making and the top-down processes of development. It is a fact that the 73rd and 74th Amendments to the Constitution followed immediately upon the macro-economic crisis of 1990–1991 and the stabilization and structural adjustments, packages administered by the International Monetary Fund and the World Bank. However, as Amartya Sen has noted, the failures in the development of educational facilities, health care provisions and environmental protection cannot be ascribed to 'overactive' government alone. The errors of commission (state-led allocation of resources, public investment in manufacturing and services) are to be viewed together with the errors of omission (under investments in health, nutrition and education). The basic issue, therefore, is not that of 'over governance' or 'under governance' but that of the quality of governance.[21]

The constitutional mandate for democratic governance at the local (village, municipal) level as embodied in the 73rd and 74th Constitutional Amendments acknowledges that:

1. centralized governance stifled local initiative and participation
2. top-down planning led to a dependency among the citizens, and that growth continued to exclude large groups in society (women, dalits and tribal)

3. good governance (accountable, transparent and corruption free) is only possible when citizens have opportunities to participate in and practice democratic decision-making as such decisions affect the quality of their lives.

The New Mantra – 'Think Global and Act Local'

The factor that determines whether governance is local or not is the extent to which the local population is involved in the steering, that is, in determining the direction according to their local needs, problems and priorities and the level to which they are the beneficiaries of the governance. Therefore, the government is not merely about governing, but also about growing into the larger concept of governance. This includes a variety of actors and factors at local as well as national and international levels. At the grassroots level, community groups, civil society and NGOs also engineer collective action to address local problems with a local touch. What is local about local governance? It needs not be the actor but rather the needs, interests, priorities, participation, control and well-being of the local population. It is important to have this in mind. For effective local governance, decentralization policies, strategies, legal frameworks, programmes and activities must be conceived from two planes (Figure 2.1)[22]:

1. The *vertical plane*, involving the transfer of authority, functions, responsibilities and resources from central government to local government structures

2. The *horizontal plane*, involving the empowerment of grassroot communities to enable them to determine, plan, manage and implement their socio-politico-economic development.

Figure 2.1

Vertical and Horizontal Decentralization[23]

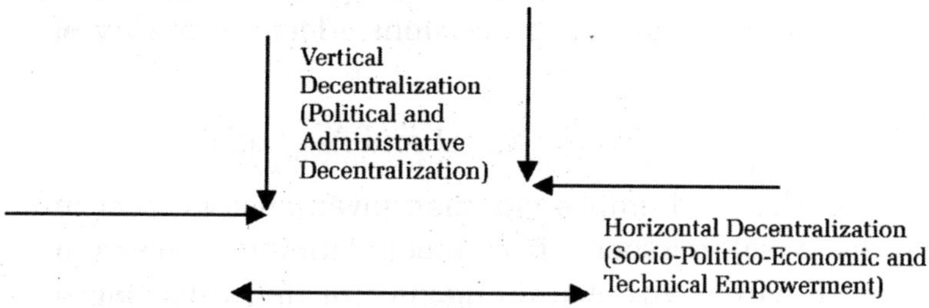

Development through Decentralized Local Governance

Rapid human development and strong local democracy go hand in hand (UNDP, 2000).[24] The 21st century is the century of hope, aspirations and dreams, which seem to be achievable in the context of globalization as it provides innumerable opportunities to all. In the process of development, it is necessary to invite participation and give people the power of decision-making. This is a booster doze to elevate people and empower them. Decentralization of power brings decision-making closer to the people and therefore yields programmes and services that better address local needs. The challenge is to ensure that all stakeholders can and will voice their opinions. Community participation and boosting grassroots development plays a key role in the sustainability of programmes and quality of life improvements. Bringing the stakeholders together to define priorities for projects and programmes increases interest and sense of ownership, this in turn promotes sustainability (UNDP, 2002).[25]

A municipality in Brazil, Belo Horizonte, formed a municipal health council bringing together stakeholders from the community, the local and central governments. Consequently, the council was better able to prioritize the needs of the community, improve communication with all stakeholders including the private sector and increase allocated resources from the Ministry of Health in exchange for a stronger system of accountability. These achievements ultimately led to the improvement in immunization rates and lower infant mortality – top priorities defined by the council. Supporting open dialogue and participation between the local government and civil society can ensure improved self-reliance. The Local Initiative Facility for Urban Environment (LIFE) programme in Tanzania has helped strengthen the link between civil society and local governance institutions and thereby improving local capacity to solve key development problems. In industrial countries, special purpose agencies or bodies deliver a wide range of metropolitan and regional public services, including education, health, planning, recreation, and environmental protection.

Decentralization and community-driven management acquire special importance in the context of the ongoing process of globalization and associated economic reforms. While the process of globalization acts in ways in which the market acquires supremacy to the detriment of people who lose control over their livelihood patterns as well as other choices, the process of decentralization could act as a countervailing force enabling people to acquire control over decisions that influence their lives in critical areas (UNDP, 2000: 1).[26]

Indian Government since 1992 constitutionally is supporting the cause of promoting local governance but what is more important is that local bodies should also pay heed to the concerns of inclusiveness, accountability and effectiveness. Local bodies need to be seen as institutions of self-governance not as 'delivery mechanisms'. Elected local government institutions must be helped to become vehicles for social transformation, articulating the felt needs of the community, especially those of women and marginalized groups.

To realize this we need to revamp the whole system by rearranging the administrative structures, modifying the procedures and introducing new paradigms of governance. This will help the units of local governments as these will serve as their weapons to fight for the development of their village. States such as Kerala and Madhya Pradesh have placed line departments in several sectors under the control of local bodies, a factor that has contributed to the resilience of their decentralization initiatives. The United Nations Development Programme (UNDP) as a whole and the Institutional Development Group of the Bureau for Development Policy in particular have highlighted the integral role of good governance and decentralization in the development process and have continually provided support to decentralization programmes worldwide.

India Heading the Way

The constitutional mandate given to PRIs in 1992 through 73rd Constitutional Amendment is just an icing on the cake. This land has since time immemorial given support for the growth and strengthening of village governing institutions. We can claim to be the world's biggest decentralized democracy. We are now heading towards a new start and look forward to address global challenges under global circumstances with the help of local wherewithal. Perceptions about India among global investors are very favourable. These developments suggest that our economy is now at a point when it can achieve sustained economic expansion that has the potential to bring significant improvement in the lives of our people.[27] The argument for greater devolution in India is based on the experience of states such as Kerala,

Madhya Pradesh, Karnataka and Uttar Pradesh, which demonstrate that the transfer of funds, functions and functionaries is the key to more successful decentralization. It is imperative to strengthen decentralization from below, so that voices of the poor could carry weight in village assemblies and ward council meetings. Apart from social mobilization, this can be accomplished by strengthening community networks and institutions.

Inclusive Growth through Inclusive Governance

Inclusive growth is a growth process which yields broad-based benefits and ensures equality of opportunity for all. A major weakness in our economy is that the growth is not perceived as being sufficiently inclusive for many groups, especially SCs, STs and minorities. Gender inequality also remains a pervasive problem and some of the structural changes taking place have an adverse effect on women. The lack of inclusiveness is borne out by data on several dimensions of performance.

Therefore, the Eleventh Plan is aimed at bringing about major improvements in governance, which would make government-funded programmes in critical areas more effective and efficient. The best possible way of achieving this objective may be by involving communities in both the design and implementation of such programmes, although such involvement may vary from sector to sector. Experience shows that civil society organizations (CSOs) can work with PRIs to improve the effectiveness of these programmes. For achieving the vision of the eleventh plan, it is extremely important to experiment with programme design to give more flexibility to decision-making at the local level.

In the continuous process of globalizing world, the issue of governance assumes greater significance because a lot depends on the efficacy of a government to implement the targeted poverty alleviation programme and managing the economy. The government indicates certain methods that societies may use for distributing power and managing public resources and problems. But the governance should have a human face so that necessary enabling environment is created for human development and eradication of human deprivation. In India's rural economy, the government panchayat bodies are supposed to perform this dual role of decentralized and human development for the welfare of the people (Chatterjee and Ghosh, 2003).[28]

Strengthening the Gram Sabha is an important step in this direction. Gram Sabha serves as the empowered and proximate forum for local democracy, especially in regions characterized by a dispersed pattern of settlement it is an essential step. The Panchayat Extension to Scheduled Areas Act, 1996, has taken steps in this direction, by making the Gram Sabha the cornerstone of people's empowerment. The momentum of this initiative needs to be built upon to ensure that the village assembly/ward council becomes the centre-piece of local democracy. The Eleventh Finance Commission also recommended strengthening the finances of local bodies (panchayats and municipal bodies).

Decentralization: Not a Panacea for all Ills

Although decentralization has brought spiralling changes in the lives of the people at the grassroots, it is not devoid of pitfalls. The transfer of power to the units of local governance not always brings positive alterations. The pragmatic inspection of the process reveals the fact that there are many challenges when it comes to implementation and functions of the local governance. Decentralization cannot be a panacea for all ills. However, if the decentralization of power is combined with strategic changes and meticulous efforts and also real political will on the part of leaders it can create wonders.

Richard Crook[29] has tried to capture some of the ill effects of decentralization experiment and maintains that decentralized governance is unlikely to produce more pro-poor governmental performance, in fact he is of the opinion that it has many a time failed to encourage participation and also have been neither representative nor spontaneous. He also speaks of unaccountable decentralization processes in various countries and criticizes elite capture of elected local governments.

The idea behind sharing the power at the grassroots is basically associated with cherishing the Greek dream of direct democracy where each man is part of the democratic process. Each man is endowed with some legitimate opportunities, rights and powers to be a part of the decision-making exercise. This is an important measure to keep men from all strata in the mainstream so each one gets at least a single opportunity to be the survivor in the globalizing and competitive world. However as discussed earlier, decentralization process is benefiting the targeted section of the society and if it is moving with right context and right will, then J.S. Mill's dream of local governance can be realized in reality.

Good Governance through Local Governance

Human conglomerations since ages have been trying to improve their life quantitatively as well as qualitatively. It is an untiring effort undertaken on the part of mankind all over the globe. Therefore, since time immemorial, humans have been longing to better the way they govern themselves and their peripheral environment. Earlier, governance was a much narrow concept confined to the scope of maintenance of law and order or tax collection and distribution. From police state to welfare state to corporate or a facilitator state, this concept has been taken to a new level. Here, an attempt is made to explore the idea of good governance in the context of globalization.

The word *governance* has its origin in the Greek language and it refers to steering. Simply put, governance means the process of decision-making and the process by which decisions are implemented (or not implemented). As an act of steering a people's socio-politico-economic development, governance is a multifaceted compound situation of institutions, systems, structures, processes, procedures, practices, relationships and leadership behaviour in the exercise of social, political, economic, and managerial/administrative authority in the running of public or private affairs. Good governance is the exercise of this authority with the participation, interest, and livelihood of the governed as the driving force.[30] Governance is also broadly defined as the system of values, policies and institutions by which a society organizes collective decision-making and action related to political, economic and socio-cultural and environmental affairs through the interaction of the state, civil society and the private sector. Governance comprises the complex mechanisms, processes and institutions through which citizens and groups articulate their interests, mediate their differences and exercise their legal rights and obligations.[31]

Today, the entire concept of governance needs to be revamped. Catchwords such as local government, good governance, new public management, contracting out, social capital, people-centred development, community-driven management and development, citizen's participation, capacity building and social audit are gaining importance. Good governance today has become a foremost requirement of public as well as private bodies. In the public sphere, it demands utmost attention as it is a tool to tackle many global and local challenges. People across the globe, stricken with abject poverty, lack of facilities and absence of voicing their demands, today are crying for a system of governance that can provide their voice and choice: a ventilation. According to the former UN Secretary-General, Kofi Annan, 'Good governance is perhaps the single most important factor in eradicating poverty and promoting development'.

Two Paradoxes: Global and Local

We today identify two paradoxical trends running simultaneously and affecting our lives. These are globalization and localization. In Japan, global corporations tailored products and marketing to particular local circumstances to meet variations in consumer demand. Robertson (1992) goes even further in seeing globalization or interpenetration of the global and local as the defining feature of the global society, evident not merely in business, but also in many other aspects of social life. Globalization is the process by which a single global field has come into being but it is not only component part of the global field, but also other components that include particular localities.

While globalization shrinks the economic space of the state, the latter must rely on the political and cultural arenas to maintain or increase its domestic sovereignty. Governments have increasingly reinvented themselves less in terms of powers and hierarchy and more in terms of partnerships and collaborations. We find the following trends in this context[32]: institutional distinction between the public, nonprofit, private sectors, federal, state and local government becoming fuzzy, muddy and gray government – flatter and horizontal devolution – local government an instrument of decentralization, democracy and good governance.

To achieve good governance, 'democratic decentralization at the grassroots is envisaged as the most important strategy to make democracy meaningful and achieve the goals of a responsive, corruption free, effective and transparent administration and delivery of services to rural and urban population (Jain, 2005).[33] According to Robert Ebel, 'The western world sees decentralization as an alternative to provide public services in the most cost-effective way. Developing countries are pursing decentralization reforms to counter economic inefficiencies, macroeconomic instability, and ineffective governance'.[34] Similarly, Aldous Huxley says that 'the political road to a better society is the road of decentralization and responsible self-government'. Decentralization is also a check against a leviathan government. These factors have also led to debate over the concept of good governance. Decentralization has come to be widely regarded as an important instrument for supporting the factors needed to create good local governance and promote local development.

Good governance is in essence about being able to provide equal opportunities to people in socio-economic and political life, being responsive to people's need, being able to meet basic needs of people and fair and accountable in dealings (Gupta, 2004).[35]

According to the World Bank, good governance is the manner in which power is exercised in the management of a country's economic and social resources for the development. Good governance is synonymous with sound development management. To the World Bank, the concept has four components which are as follows:

1. Public sector management
2. Legal framework for development
3. Accountability
4. Information (transparency)

Significance of Good Governance

Good governance is absolutely necessary in order to provide the greatest good to the greatest number of people. Good governance has increasingly become a catchphrase. It is being widely used by different international agencies such as the UNDP, the World Bank, the Organization for Economic Cooperation and Development (OECD), and the Commission on Global Governance (CGG).

Good governance means 'governing well', that is, clean governance to achieve the anticipated goals and objectives of the public and the government (Dwivedi and Mishra, 2004: 722).[36] According to Halder, a good governance should not only take care of ensuring maximum 'opportunity' or 'liberty' to the citizens for full flowering of their innate capabilities, which have social relevance in a given set of conditions, defined by the existing level of literacy and the economic circumstances, but should also ensure the favourable atmosphere for changing the existing set of conditions for a better one (Halder, 2004: 1050).[37]

The concept of good governance is much larger than mere administrative reforms in the conventional sense of the term. In fact, it covers much more ground and substance than administrative reforms. It looks at the functioning of the given segment of the society from the point of view of its acknowledged stakeholders and beneficiaries and customers. It must have firm moorings to certain moral values and principles.

The foremost test of good governance is the respect for rule of law. As the saying goes, howsoever high a person may be, the law is above him and has to be considered supreme. The governance must be based on rule of law. Every lawfully established government must govern according to the laws of the land. The principle of subsidiarity must become the guiding principle in the governance. This would imply doing

Box 2.1

Five Principles of Good Governance

The Five Good Governance Principles	*The UNDP Principles and related UNDP text on which they are based*
1. Legitimacy and Voice	Participation: all men and women should have a voice in decision-making, either directly or through legitimate intermediate institutions that represent their intention. Such broad participation is built on freedom of association and speech, as well as capacities to participate constructively.
2. Direction	Strategic vision: leaders and the public have a broad and long-term perspective on good governance and human development, along with a sense of what is needed for such development. There is also an understanding of the historical, cultural and social complexities in which that perspective is grounded.
3. Performance	Responsiveness: institutions and processes try to serve all stakeholders. Effectiveness and efficiency – processes and institutions produce results that meet needs while making the best use of resources.
4. Accountability	Accountability: decision-makers in government, the private sector and civil society organizations are accountable to the public, as well as to institutional stakeholders. This accountability differs depending on the organizations and whether the decision is internal or external.
	Transparency: transparency is built on the free flow of information. processes, institutions and information are directly accessible to those concerned with them, and enough information is provided to understand and monitor them.
5. Fairness	Equity: all men and women have opportunities to improve or maintain their well being.
	Rule of Low: legal frameworks should be fair and enforced impartially, particularly the laws on human rights.

Source: Note on good governance available at http://www.img.kerala. gov.in/docs/downloads/gg.pdf

Box 2.2

Characteristics of Good Governance

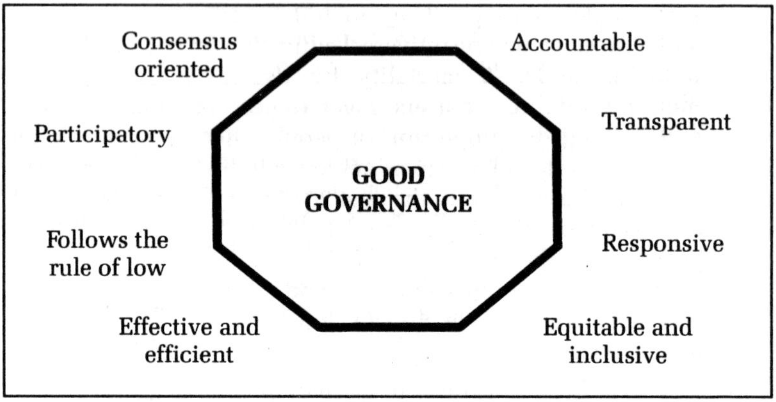

Source: What is Governance? available at http://www.unescap.org/pdd/prs/ProjectActivities/Ongoing/gg/governance.asp

things at the level at which they can be best done. Thus, as much of legislative, executive and administrative actions must be decentralized as possible (Godbole, 2001) (see Boxes 2.1 and 2.2).[38]

Notes

1. United Nations Development Programme, *Overview of Decentralization World Wide: A Stepping Stone to Improved Governance and Human Development*, 2nd International Conference on Decentralization, July 2002, http://www.cities-localgovernments.org/committees/dal/Upload/library/overviewofdecentralisationworldwide_work_2002.pdf
2. Manor, James, *The Political Economy of Democratic Decentralization*, Washington DC: The World Bank, 1999.
3. Bardhan, Pranab and Mukherjee, Dilip, *Decentralization and Local Governments in Developing Countries: Comparative Perspective*, New Delhi: Oxford University Press, 2007.
4. Mohan, Sudha, *Urban Development and New Localism*, Rawat Publications, 2005.

5. The Millennium Development Goals (MDGs) are a set of time-bound targets that express key elements of human development and have been created to guide the progress of sustainable solutions. They include halving income-poverty and hunger, achieving universal education and gender equality, reducing under—5 mortality by two-thirds and maternal mortality by three-quarters, reversing the spread of HIV/AIDS and halving the proportion of people without access to safe water. These targets are to be achieved by 2015, from their level in 1990. These MDGs in the post 2015 period have been termed as sustainable development goals 2030. Over the next fifteen years, with these new Goals that universally apply to all, countries will mobilize efforts to end all forms of poverty, fight inequalities and tackle climate change, while ensuring that no one is left behind.
6. Gupta, D.N., *Decentralization: Need for Reforms*, New Delhi: Concept Publishing House, 2004.
7. Bardhan, Pranab and Mukherjee, Dilip, op. cit.
8. Source: *Factors to Consider in Designing Decentralized Governance: Policies and Programmes to Achieve Sustainable People-Centered Development*, Management Development and Governance Division, United Nations Development Programme, New York, February 1998.
9. Ibid.
10. Manor, James, op. cit.
11. United Nations Development Programme, *Overview of Decentralization World Wide: A Stepping Stone to Improved Governance and Human Development*, 2nd International Conference on Decentralization, July 2002, http://www.cities-localgovernments.org/committees/dal/Upload/library/overviewofdecentralisationworldwide_work_2002.pdf
12. *Report* of the Administrative Reforms Commission, 2006.
13. Shah, Anwar and Shah, Sana, *Local Governments in Developing Countries*, Washington, DC: The World Bank, 2006.
14. Oates, Wallace, *Fiscal Federalism*, New York: Harcourt Brace Jovanovich, 1972.
15. Report of the Administrative Reforms Commission, 2006.
16. Shah, Anwar and Shah, Sana, op. cit.
17. Ibid.

18. United Nations Development Programme, *Decentralization in India: Challenges and Opportunities*, New Delhi, Human Development Resource Centre, 2000, http://www.in.undp.org/content/dam/india/docs/decentralisation_india_challenges_opportunities.pdf.
19. The evolution and development of PRIs is dealt in detail in the chapter on Evolution of PRIs.
20. *Engaging with Participatory Local Governance in India* presented by Satinder Sahni, PRIA, available at http://unpan1.un.org/intradoc/groups/public/documents/un/unpan013176.pdf.
21. Ibid.
22. *Local Governance Capacity-Building for Full-Range Participation: Concepts, Frameworks and Experiences in African Countries*, by John-Mary Kauzya, United Nations, August 2003.
23. Ibid.
24. United Nations Development Programme, *Decentralization in India: Challenges and Opportunities*, New Delhi: Human Development Resource Centre, 2000, http://www.in.undp.org/content/dam/india/docs/decentralisation_india_challenges_opportunities.pdf.
25. United Nations Development Programme, *Overview of Decentralization World Wide: A Stepping Stone to Improved Governance and Human Development*, 2nd International Conference on Decentralisation, July 2002, http://www.cities-localgovernments.org/committees/dal/Upload/library/overviewofdecentralisationworldwide_work_2002.pdf.
26. United Nations Development Programme, *Decentralization in India: Challenges and Opportunities*, New Delhi: Human Development Resource Centre, 2000, http://www.in.undp.org/content/dam/india/docs/decentralisation_india_challenges_opportunities.pdf.
27. *Inclusive Growth*, 11th Five Year Plan, Page 1, available at http://www.planningcommission.nic.in/plans/planrel/fiveyr/11th/11_v1/11v1_ch1.pdf.
28. Chatterjee Biswajit and Ghosh Dilip Kumar, 'Globalization and Decentralized Governance: Reflections on Panchayats in India', *Indian Journal of Public Administration*, Vol. XLIX, No. 2, April/June, 2003.

29. *Decentralization and Poverty-Alleviation in Developing countries: A Comparative Analysis or, Is West Bengal Unique?* Institute of Development Studies, Working Paper No. 130, by Richard C. Crook and Alan Sturla Sverrisson, February 2001, available at www.ntd.co.uk/idsbookshop/details.asp?id=617
30. *Local Governance Capacity-Building for Full-Range Participation: Concepts, Frameworks and Experiences in African Countries* by John-Mary Kauzya August 2003, United Nations.
31. UNDP, *Overview of Decentralization World Wide: A Stepping Stone to Improved Governance and Human Development*, 2002, http://www.cities-localgovernments.org/committees/dal/Upload/library/overviewofdecentralisationworldwide_work_2002.pdf.
32. Intersectoral Administration: Implementing Governance in 21st Century, *Administrative Change*, Vol. XXXII, No. 2 and Vol. XXXIII No.1, January/December 2005.
33. Jain, R.B. (ed.), *Globalization and Good Governance: Pressures for Constructive Reforms*, New Delhi: Deep & Deep Publications Pvt. Ltd., 2005.
34. Ebel, Robert, 'Logic of Decentralisation and Worldwide Overview,' *Talking Points*, 4 September 1998.
35. Gupta, D.N., op. cit.
36. Dwivedi, O.P. and Mishra, D.S., 'A Good Governance Model for India', *The Indian Journal of Public Administration*, Vol. LI, No. 4, October/December 2004, pp. 719–58.
37. Halder, Dilip, 'Democratic Governance Is No Panacea: The Experience of India and South Asia', *The Indian Journal of Public Administration*, Vol. L, No. 4, October/December 2004, pp. 1046–69.
38. Report of the One Man Committee on Good Governance by Dr Madhav Godbole, July 2001, available at http://maharashtracivilservice.org/cms/downloads/516b0f962943f.pdf.

3

Evolution of Panchaya[illegible] Institutions in Indi[illegible]

3

Evolution of Panchayati Raj Instituions in India

> ... each village a complete republic ... . independent for its vital wants and yet interdependent for many others in which dependence is necessity.
>
> —Gandhi's vision of village governance

India has a chequered history of Panchayati Raj starting from self-sufficient and self-governing village communities to modern-day organized village governance system in the format of Panchayati Raj Institutions or PRIs (see Figure 3.1). There is sufficient evidence to establish the fact that the institution of local self-government is almost pre-historic, and the conception of local self-government is indigenous to the Indian soil. Municipal governments have flourished in India since time immemorial.

In every village, a council of five members, generally called as the panchayat, enjoyed large executive and judicial powers. These adjudicative powers are even today exercised by Khap panchayats in northern parts of India. The Russian *Mir*, the German *Mark*, and the medieval *Manor* of England could be considered the counterparts of Indian village panchayat (Mathew, 2002: 3).[1] They were the

Figure 3.1

Genesis and Growth of Local Self-Government in India

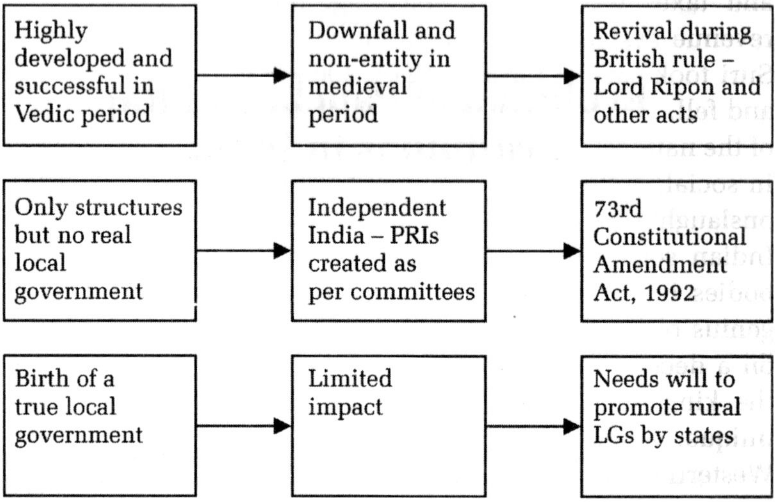

Source: Mor (2007).

pivot of administration, the centre of social life, forum for justice, an important economic force and above all, a focus of social solidarity (Mathew, 2002: 4).[2]

Therefore, Sir Charles Metcalfe called these village communities as 'little republics'. In the opinion of H. Tinker, these panchayats had members from the superior class of cultivators. In pre-British India, both caste and village panchayats existed. Caste panchayats were concerned with issues related to *jajmani*, marriage and rituals. Village panchayats consisted of elders of prominent household in a village. They were concerned primarily with adjudicating civil disputes of residents related to rights in land and administering criminal justice. They also performed regulatory functions related to village commons (grazing lands, woods and water bodies). In Majumdar's view, panchayats also collected taxes out of the produce and the government's share on behalf of the village.[3] However, the UNDP report says that responsibility for payment of tithes and taxes was, strictly speaking, not their concern; the revenue systems introduced since the times of Sher Shah Suri took care of these (UNDP, 2000).[4] While empires rose and fell, village panchayats – which formed an integral part of the national life – helped to preserve democratic traditions in social, cultural, economic and political life; survived the onslaughts of centuries of political upheavals and saved Indian society from disintegration. The existence of local bodies in ancient India is a positive proof of the inherent genius of our people to manage local affairs efficiently and on a decentralized basis. The decentralization of power in the kingdoms of the Maurya and the Gupta periods was unique. Such devolution of power was unknown to the Western world until modern times.

Vedic Era

India – the land of oldest civilization of the world – is also a pioneer in the field of village governance. The seeds of democracy were sown long before British introduced this format to India. Rishi Atri championed the idea of democracy to voice against a demon king and established the rule of the people (Athavale, 1999).[5] In ancient India Sabhas and Samitis were functional forms of governance. In the process of evolution of grassroots governance, these sabhas morphed into council of five, namely panchayat.

The word *Gramini* is referred to in the Vedas, which means leader of the village. There is a reference of 'Janapadas' in Valmiki's *Ramayana* as a kind of federation of village republics. 'Gram Sanghas' is also mentioned in the Mahabharata and Manusmriti (three kinds of settlements: Grama, Pura and Nagara) and Gram Sabha in the Buddhist Jatakas (4th or 5th BC), Kautilya's Arthashastra and

Shukracharya's Nitisar (around 1000 AD). Mention of Kumbha, Palli and Grama gives a long account of the rural communities and their existence. The references of panchayats are found in Shrutis and Smritis and to Gana and Pura in the Dharmasutras as well (Mor, 2007).[6]

The concept of local self-government is not new to our country, and there is mention of community assemblies in the Vedic texts. Around 600 BC, the territory north of the river Ganga comprising modern-day north Bihar and eastern Uttar Pradesh was under the suzerainty of small republics called Janapadas among which Licchavis were the most powerful. In these Janapadas, the affairs of the state were conducted by an assembly consisting of local chieftains.

In the post-Mauryan times as well, there existed republics of Malavas and the Kshudrakas where decisions were taken by 'sabhas'. The Greek Ambassador, Megasthenes, who visited the court of Chandragupta Maurya in 303 BC, described the city council which governed Pataliputra – comprising six committees with 30 members.

Similar participatory structures also existed in South India. In the Chola kingdom, the village council, together with its subcommittees and wards, played an important part in administration by arbitrating disputes and managing social affairs. They were also responsible for revenue collection, assessing individual contribution and negotiating the collective assessment with the king's representatives. They had virtual ownership of village waste land, with right of sale, and they were also involved in irrigation, road building and related work. Their transactions, recorded on the walls of village temples, show a vigorous community life and are a permanent memorial to the best practices in early Indian polity (ARC, 2006).

Inscriptions of Parantak I (907 AD to 949 AD) provide a good account of the manner in which local affairs were organized and it also mentions qualifications and disqualifications for membership of various village committees. The list of these qualifications testifies one fact that these village panchayats were quite egalitarian, representative or cosmopolitan bodies (Majumdar and Singh, 1997).[7] It is thus clear that in the northern as well as southern India village republics flourished and strengthened the system of local governance on this land.

Setback during the Muslim Rule

The system of village governance received a heavy set back during the reigns of Mughal emperors. The onslaught these alien rulers tarnished the administrative set up to establish and spread their rule.

Sir Jadunath Sarkar writes, 'Mughal government was highly centralized autocracy. The crown was the motive of the entire administrative machinery'. The degeneration of the robust system of local self-governance during medieval India was primarily due to the overwhelming influence of casteism and highly centralised and commandist nature of Mughal administration in India.

The Muslim rulers recognized local chiefs and zamindars as the repositories of local authority, to the exclusion of the people. The villages and towns of the Mughal Empire enjoyed parochial self-government rather than local autonomy. The people who do not possess political freedom and powers of self-taxation for national purposes cannot be said to enjoy local autonomy. The office of 'Kotwal' was developed as the keystone of the municipal administration and 'his functions in connection with the town in his charge were, at least in theory, the most comprehensive conceivable being in certain respects even wider than those of the municipal bodies of the present day'. Between the breakdown of the Mughal Empire and the coming of the British, there was complete anarchy and military despotism in most parts of the country.

Under the British Rule

When India was colonized, there occurred a sharp break from the tradition. The form adopted during the British rule was an admixture of the British and continental patterns. The village panchayat system suffered a deliberate decay under the rule of the East India Company. In the early British period however, they still remained a primary unit of the administration. Therefore, Mountstuart Elphinstone, the first governor of Bombay, said that these village republics were miniatures of the state (Majumdar and Singh, 1997).[8]

The present structure of local self-government institutions took shape in 1688 when the British established a Municipal Corporation at Madras, which was followed by the creation of similar bodies at Bombay and Calcutta (1726). Comprising a mayor and a majority of British-born councillors, these corporations were basically units of administration enjoying considerable judicial powers. During the next 150 years, municipal bodies were created in several mufassil towns, although their functions remained confined to conservancy, road repairs, lighting and a few other sundry items (ARC, 2006).

The role of panchayats as institutions administering justice was eliminated by the British legislations in 1860 such as the Indian Penal Code (IPC), Criminal Procedure Code (CrPC), Contract Act and so on.

The panchayats had never been the priority of the British rulers. The rulers were interested in the creation of 'controlled' local bodies, which could help them in their trading interests by collecting taxes for them. When the colonial administration came under severe financial pressure after the 1857 uprising, the remedy sought was decentralization in terms of transferring responsibility for road and public works to local bodies. However, the thrust of this 'compelled' decentralization was with respect to municipal administration.

Viceroy Lord Mayo's Resolution of 1870 for decentralization of power to bring about administrative efficiency in meeting people's demand and to add to the finances of colonial regime gave the needed impetus to the development of local institutions. It was in the wake of this resolution that the first significant step to revive the traditional village panchayat system in Bengal was taken in 1870 through the Bengal Chowkidari Act (ISS, 2000: 4).[9] It was a landmark in the evolution of colonial policy towards local government.

The Famine Commission of 1880 had pointed to the absence of local bodies as a major impediment in reaching relief supplies to the famine-stricken people and had recommended the need to expand self-government to the villages as well.

The real benchmark in the field of local government was the government policy on decentralization presented by a Liberal Lord Ripon who, in his famous resolution on local self-government on 18 May 1882, recognized the twin considerations of local government as under:

1. Administrative Efficiency
2. Political Education

The reforms introduced by Lord Rippon created the foundation of a robust system of local self-governance in India. Since India already had experiences of self-governance through local panchayats, these newly created structures quickly took firm roots and contributed immensely to building enduring democratic institutions (Goel and Shalini, 2003).[10]

The Ripon resolution focused on towns, provided for local bodies consisting of a large majority of elected non-official members and presided over by a non-official chairperson. This resolution met with resistance from colonial administrators. The progress of local self-government was tardy with only half-hearted steps taken in setting up municipal bodies. Rural decentralization remained a neglected area of administrative reforms.

However, an effective structure for rural areas came up with the enactment of the Bengal Local Self-Government Act, 1885, which led to the establishment of district local boards across the entire territory of the then Bengal province.

The Royal Commission on Decentralization (1907), under the chairmanship of C.E.H. Hobhouse, recognized the importance of panchayats at the village level. It concluded t at chiefly due to their unrepresentative character and inadequate powers, these bodies had not been a success (Goel and Shalini, 2003).[11] The commission recommended that it is most desirable, alike in the interests of decentralization and in order to associate the people with the local tasks of administration that an attempt should be made to constitute and develop village panchayats for the administration of local village affairs.

But, the Montagu–Chelmsford Reforms (1919) brought local self-government as a provincial transferred subject, under the domain of Indian ministers in the provinces. Due to organizational and fiscal constraints, the reform was unable to make panchayat institutions truly democratic and vibrant. However, the most significant development of this period was the establishment of village panchayats in a number of provinces, which were no longer mere ad-hoc judicial tribunal, but representative institutions symbolizing the corporate character of the village and having a wide jurisdiction with respect to civic matters. By 1925, eight provinces had passed panchayat acts and by 1926, six native states had also passed panchayat laws.

The provincial autonomy under the Government of India Act, 1935, marked the evolution of panchayats in India. Popularly elected governments in provinces enacted legislations to further democratize institutions of local self-government. But the system of responsible government at the grassroots level was least responsible. D.P. Mishra, the then minister for local self-government under the Government of India, was of the view that local bodies became the most inefficient functional bodies in India (Venkatarangaiah and Pattabhiram, 1969).[12]

In spite of various committees such as the Royal Commission on Decentralization (1907), the report of Montagu–Chelmsford on Constitutional Reforms (1919) and the Government of India Resolution (1918), a hierarchical administrative structure based on supervision and control evolved. The administrator became the focal point of rural governance. The British were not concerned with decentralized democracy but were aiming for colonial objectives (Venkatarangaiah and Pattabhiram, 1969).

The Indian National Congress, from the 1920 to 1947, emphasized the issue of Swaraj and organized movements for independence under the leadership of Mahatma Gandhi. As a result, the task of preparing any sort of blueprint for the local level was neglected. There was no consensus among the top leaders regarding the status and role to be assigned to the institutions of rural local self-government; rather there were divergent views on the subject. On the one hand, Gandhi favoured Village Swaraj and strengthening the village panchayats to the fullest extent and on the other hand, Dr B.R. Ambedkar opposed this idea. He believed that the village represented regressive India, a source of oppression. The model state hence had to build safeguards against such social oppression and the only way it could be done was through the adoption of the parliamentary model of politics (The World Bank, 2000).[13]

During the drafting of the Constitution of India, PRIs were placed in the non-justiciable part of the Constitution – the Directive Principles of State Policy – as Article 40. The Article reads, 'the State shall take steps to organise village panchayats and endow them with such powers and authority as may be necessary to enable them to function as units of self-government'. Under Article 246, the state legislatures are empowered to enact any law regarding any aspect of local self-government. In the four decades since the adoption of the Constitution, PRIs have travelled from the non-justiciable part of the Constitution to one where, through a separate amendment, a whole new status has been added to their history (Bajpai and Verma, 1995).[14]

Beginning of a New Saga: Post-Independence Period

In the years that followed independence, the national leadership was overwhelmed with state capitalist, state control and state planning model of the Soviet Russia. This naturally was reflected in the national government's policy options and policy choices. It also inadvertently defied the idea of widespread people's participation in the planning and decision-making process. The worst part of independence year and following decade was that despite giant centrally funded and designed programmes for welfare of the people, because of distant and sparing people's participation, British-styled centralized approach and lack of both political and bureaucratic will, all efforts of involving people remained mostly on paper.

Community Development Programme and National Extension Service

Community Development Programme (CDP) in 1952 and National Extension Service (NES) in 1953 were introduced to implement CDP in the country. The introduction of CDP was a major step for bringing about economic development and social welfare in rural India (Goel and Shalini, 2003).[15] In compliance with the provisions of the Directive Principles of State Policy pertaining to establishment of village panchayats as units of local self-government, an ambitious rural sector initiative, called as the Community Development Programme, was launched in 1952. Its main thrust was on securing socio-economic transformation of village life through people's own democratic and cooperative organizations with the government providing technical services, supply and credit. Under this programme, 100 to 150 villages formed a community development block, and the participation of the whole community was the key element of this experiment which strengthened the foundation of grassroots democracy. In 1953, the NES was introduced, which was an amplified version of the CDP and aimed at transferring scientific and technical knowledge to agricultural, animal husbandry and rural craft sectors. The underlying theme was an extension of innovative pilot projects. While the programme did not have any content of elected democratic institutions since they were run by government functionaries with the help of ad hoc semi-popular bodies such as Vikas Mandal and Prakhand Samiti, yet in the midst of the euphoria prevailing immediately after independence in the country, they – to a great extent – caught the attention of the rural masses (ARC, 2006).

However, these programmes did not encourage the people much, as government functionaries engaged were apathetic and corrupt. Favouritism, wastage and malpractices resulted in tarnishing the image of the programmes. After the failure of the first and second five-year plans, which aimed to gain people's participation in the development process, the Planning Commission also strongly advocated making the panchayats as the nucleus of the planning and implementation of schemes of the CDP and NES. Hence, committees were constituted by various authorities to advise the centre on different aspects of decentralization.

The Balwant Rai Mehta Committee

In 1957, the Balwant Rai Mehta Committee studied the Community Development Projects and the NES and assessed the extent to which the movement had succeeded in utilizing local initiatives and in creating institutions to ensure continuity in the process of improving economic and social conditions in rural areas. The committee held that community development would only be deep and enduring when the community was involved in the planning, decision-making and implementation process (GoI, 1957).[16] The suggestions were as follows (Kashyap, 1989)[17]:

- an early establishment of elected local bodies and devolution of necessary resources, power and authority to them,
- that the basic unit of democratic decentralization was at the block/samiti level since the area or jurisdiction of the local body should neither be too large nor too small. The block was large enough for efficiency and economy of administration, and small enough for sustaining a sense of involvement in the citizens,
- such body must not be constrained by too much control by the government or government agencies,

- the body must be constituted for five years by indirect elections from the village panchayats,
- its functions should cover the development of agriculture in all its aspects, the promotion of local industries and others,
- access to services such as drinking water, road building, and others, and
- the higher level body, Zilla Parishad, would play an advisory role.

The Panchayati Raj structure did not develop the requisite democratic momentum and failed to cater to the needs of rural development. Probably, government was too busy with focus on handling issues of international and neighbour politics than domestic and local politics. It was also not a fashionable idea even in the West then. There are also other reasons for such an outcome which included political and bureaucratic resistance at the state level to share power and resources with local level institutions, domination of local elites over the major share of the benefits of welfare schemes, lack of capability at the local level and lack of political will.

K. Santhanam Committee on PRI Finance

One of the prime areas of concern in this long debate on PRIs was fiscal decentralization. The K. Santhanam Committee was appointed to look solely at the issue of PRI finance, in 1963. The fiscal capacity of PRIs tends to be limited, as rich resources of revenue are pre-empted by higher levels of government, and issue is still debated today. The committee was asked to determine issues related to sanctioning of grants to PRIs by the state government, evolving mutual financial relations between the three tiers of PRIs, gifts and donation, handing over revenue in full or part to PRIs. The committee recommended the following (Rai, 2001)[18]:

- panchayats should have special powers to levy special tax on land revenues and home taxes, etc.
- people should not be burdened with too many demands (taxes),
- all grants and subventions at the state level should be mobilized and sent in a consolidated form to various PRIs, and
- a Panchayati Raj Finance Corporation should be set up to look into the financial resource of PRIs at all levels, provide loans and financial assistance to these grass-roots-level governments and also provide non-financial requirements of villages.

These issues have been debated over the last six decades and have also been taken up by the State Finance Commissions, which are required to select taxes for assignment and sharing, to identify the principles for such sharing and assignment, to determine the level of grants and to recommend the final distribution of state's transfers to local authorities.

First Administrative Reforms Commission

In 1969, the first Administrative Reforms Commission, in its report on State Administration, recommended that the main executive organ of the Panchayati Raj system should be located at the district level in the form of Zilla Parishad and not at the block level as Panchayat Samiti. It was of the view that the Zilla Parishad would be in a better position to take a composite view of the resources and needs of the entire district and thus will be able to formulate a plan for the area. The commission also believed that due to paucity of resources, it was difficult to sustain a well-equipped administrative and development machinery at the level of a block (ARC, 2006).

Ashok Mehta Committee

With the coming of the Janata Party into power at the centre in 1977, a serious view was taken of the weaknesses in the functioning of Panchayati Raj (GoI, 1978).[19] It was decided to appoint a high-level committee under the chairmanship of Ashok Mehta to examine and suggest measures to strengthen PRIs. The committee had to evolve an effective decentralized system of development for PRIs. They made the following recommendations (Kashyap, 1989)[20]:

- the district is a viable administrative unit for which planning, coordination and resource allocation are feasible and technical expertise available,
- PRIs as a two-tier system, with Mandal Panchayat at the base and Zilla Parishad at the top,
- PRIs are capable of planning for themselves with the resources available to them,
- district planning should take care of the urban–rural continuum,
- representation of SCs and STs in the election to PRIs on the basis of their population,
- four-year term of PRIs,
- participation of political parties in elections, and
- any financial devolution should be committed to accepting that much of the developmental functions at the district level would be played by the panchayats.

The states of Karnataka, Andhra Pradesh and West Bengal passed new legislation based on this report. However, the flux in politics at the state level did not allow these institutions to develop their own political dynamics.

A number of committees were formed between 1978 and 1986 to look into various aspects of strengthening the local self-government institutions such as the committees under C.H. Hanumantha Rao, G.V.K. Rao and L.M. Singhvi, only minor suggestions were made for any change in the ideas/structures proposed by the Ashok Mehta Committee (ARC, 2006).

G.V.K. Rao Committee

The G.V.K. Rao Committee was appointed to once again look at various aspects of the PRIs. The committee was of the opinion that a total view of rural development must be taken in which PRIs must play a central role in handling people's problems. It recommended the following suggestions (The World Bank, 2000)[21]:

- PRIs have to be activated and provided with all the required support to become effective organizations
- PRIs at the district level and below should be assigned the work of planning, implementation and monitoring of rural development programmes
- the BDO should be the spinal cord of the rural development process.

L.M. Singhvi Committee

The L.M. Singhvi Committee studied Panchayati Raj at length. The Gram Sabha was considered as the base of a decentralized democracy and PRIs viewed as institutions of self-governance, which would actually facilitate the participation of the people in the process of planning and development. In a nutshell, it recommended the following suggestions (Rai, 2001)[22]:

- local self-government should be constitutionally recognized, protected and preserved by the inclusion of new chapter in the Constitution
- noninvolvement of political parties in panchayat elections

The suggestion of giving panchayats constitutional status was opposed by the Sarkaria Commission, but the idea, however, gained momentum in the late 1980s especially because of the endorsement by the late Prime Minister Rajiv Gandhi, who introduced the 64th Constitutional Amendment Bill in 1989 in the Lok Sabha – the lower house of parliament. But it got defeated in the Rajya Sabha as nonconvincing. He lost the general elections as well. In 1989, the National Front introduced the 74th Constitutional Amendment Bill, which could not become an act because of the dissolution of the Ninth Lok Sabha. All these suggestions and recommendations and means of strengthening PRIs were considered while formulating the new constitutional amendment act.

64th and 65th Constitutional Amendment Bills, 1989

The next landmark in decentralized governance occurred with the 64th and 65th Constitutional Amendment Bills introduced in July 1989 by the government of Rajiv Gandhi. During the period, panchayats found a renewed interest and place in the policy circles. The basic provisions of the bills proposed then were:

1. it should be mandatory for all states to set up PRIs/Urban Local Bodies (ULBs)
2. the elections to be conducted by the Election Commission
3. tenure of PRIs/ULBs to be five years and, if dissolved before time, fresh elections should be held within six months
4. all seats (except those meant for the representatives of other institutions) to be filled through direct elections
5. reservation of seats to be made for SCs/STs/women

6. local bodies to be entrusted with more functions, for example, minor irrigation, soil conservation, bio-gas, health and benefits to SCs/STs
7. planning and budgeting systems be introduced at the panchayat level
8. the state legislature to authorize PRIs/ULBs to levy taxes/tolls and fees
9. a separate commission to review the local body finances
10. PRI/ULB accounts to be audited by the Comptroller and Auditor General (CAG).

The bills could however not be passed in the Rajya Sabha (ARC, 2006).

In 1990, a combined Constitution Amendment Bill, covering both PRIs and ULBs, was tabled in parliament. It was a skeleton legislation that left the details to be crafted by the state governments in their state enactments; even matters concerning elections were left completely to the discretion of the state governments. With the dissolution of the government, this bill too lapsed (ARC, 2006).

Finally, in 1992, after synthesizing important features of the earlier exercises on this subject, the government drafted and introduced the 73rd and 74th Amendments Bills in parliament, which were passed in 1993. These introduced new Parts IX and IXA in the Indian Constitution containing Articles 243 to 243ZG and also added 11th and 12th Schedules (ARC, 2006).

The 73rd Constitutional Amendment Act

The passage of the Constitution (73rd Amendment) Act, 1992, marked a new era in the federal democratic set-up of the country and has also provided constitutional status to the PRIs (see Table 3.1).

Table 3.1

Provisions of the 73rd Amendment Act

Mandatory	*Optional*
2- to 3-Tier Structure	Direct Election of GP Chairperson
Direct Elections	Role and Scope of Gram Sabha
Reservation for Weaker Sections	Powers and Functions of Each Tier
Fixed Tenure	Financial Devolution
State Finance Commission	Maintenance and Audit of Accounts
State Election Commission	Composition and Functions of DPC
District Planning Committees	Reservation to Adhyaksha's Post
	At GP, TP and ZP Levels by Rotation

Source: Goel and Shalini (2003).

The idea that produced the 73rd Amendment was not a response to pressure from the grassroots, but to an increasing recognition that the institutional initiatives of the preceding decade had not delivered, that the extent of rural poverty was still much too large and thus the existing structure of government needed to be reformed. It is interesting to note that this idea evolved from the centre and state governments. It was a political drive to see PRIs as a solution to the governmental crises that India was experiencing. The Constitutional (73rd Amendment) Act, passed in 1992 by the Narasimha Rao Government, came into force on 24 April 1993. It was meant to provide constitutional sanction to establish 'democracy at the grassroots level as it is at the state level or national level'. Its main features are as follows (Thomas Issac and Franke, 2000)[23]:

- The Gram Sabha or village assembly as a deliberative body to decentralized governance has been envisaged as the foundation of the Panchayati Raj system.
- A uniform three-tier structure of panchayats at village (Gram Panchayat, GP), intermediate (Panchayat Samiti, PS) and district (Zilla Parishad, ZP) levels.

- All the seats in a panchayat at every level are to be filled by elections from respective territorial constituencies.
- Not less than one-third of the total seats for membership as well as office of chairpersons of each tier has to be reserved for women.
- Reservations for weaker castes and tribes (SCs and STs) have to be provided at all levels in proportion to their population in the panchayats.
- To supervise, direct and control the regular and smooth elections to panchayats, a State Election Commission has to be constituted in every state and UT.
- The act has ensured constitution of a State Finance Commission in every state/UT, for every five years, to suggest measures to strengthen finances of PRIs.
- To promote bottom-up planning, the District Planning Committee in every district has been accorded constitutional status.
- An indicative list of 29 items has been included in the Eleventh Schedule of the Constitution. Panchayats are expected to play an effective role in planning and implementation of works related to these 29 items.

Extension to the Scheduled Areas

As the provisions of the Constitution (73rd Amendment) Act did not apply to the scheduled areas located in the eight states – Andhra Pradesh, Madhya Pradesh, Rajasthan, Gujarat, Maharashtra, Himachal Pradesh, Orissa and Bihar – vide clause (i) of Article 244 of the Constitution, the parliament extended the 73rd Amendment Act to these areas on 24 December 1996 by legislating the Panchayats (Extension to the Scheduled Areas) Act, 1996. The Extension Act is notable for the vast powers given to the tribal local bodies (ISS, 2000).[24]

Present Scenario

At present, there are about 3 million elected representatives at all levels of the PRIs, of which one-third are women. These members represent more than 2.4 lakh Gram Panchayats, about 6,000 intermediate level tier and more than 500 district panchayats. Spread over the length and breadth of the country, the new panchayats cover about 96 per cent of India's more than 5.8 lakh villages and nearly 99.6 per cent of rural population. This is the largest experiment in decentralization of governance in the history of humanity.

The Constitution visualizes panchayats as institutions of self-governance. However, giving due consideration to the federal structure of our polity, most of the financial powers and authorities to be endowed on panchayats have been left at the discretion of concerned state legislatures. Consequently, the powers and functions vested in PRIs vary from state to state. These provisions combine representative and direct democracy into a synergy and are expected to result in an extension and deepening of democracy in India. Hence, panchayats have journeyed from an institution within the culture of India to attain constitutional status.

The number of village panchayats in the country as on 1 December 2006 was 2,32,913, which included 6,094 Panchayat Samitis and 537 Zilla Parishads. The total number of representatives elected to these bodies was 28,28,779, out of which 10,38,989 (36.7%) were women (ARC, 2006).

The Real Picture

Consequent upon the 73rd Constitutional Amendment as well as the Supreme Court's rulings which effectively mandate that local authorities are also to be treated as 'Government or State', the PRIs have acquired substantial legitimacy, are recognized as an instrument of the government and have created participatory structures of grassroots democracy for the rural people. Creation of constitutional bodies such as the State Election Commission and the State Finance Commission has also given permanency and stability to these institutions. However, most panchayats continue to be treated as agencies of the state for implementation of prescribed schemes, even though essential services such as provision of drinking water, rural sanitation, preventive health and primary education are accepted as their legitimate core functions. Moreover, the PRIs have a varied menu of potential taxes such as on professions, entertainment, tolls and user charges, but remain crippled by the lack of elastic revenue sources. Internal revenue mobilization remained at only 4.17 per cent of the total revenue of panchayats at all levels in 23 states during 1990–1991 to 1997–1998. In a few states such as Bihar, Rajasthan, Manipur and Sikkim, it was 'nil' during this period. Although the 11th and 12th Finance Commissions have provided untied grants to these institutions, their financial capacity remains suspect. As a result, PRIs exist as overstructured but underempowered organizations, boasting of constitutional status but suffering from the lack of effective devolution of powers and functions from the state governments (ARC, 2006).

The trajectory of the development of PRIs in India has been a journey defined by multifarious ideas that have emerged at the national and international level in governance discourse. These local self-governing bodies could not flourish in the aftermath of national independence, primarily because of extraordinary influence of socialist ideology and insistence of centralized planning. Cosmetic changes were introduced over the next few decades to establish and strengthen PRIs in India, albeit with little success. It was only after the pronouncement of new economic policy in 1991, India realized that her polity too needed an overhaul.

Table 3.2

Few Specifics about PRIs

Towards realizing the vision of Mahatma Gandhi of every village being a republic through three-tier system of Panchayati Raj.
2,32,278 panchayats at village level; 6,022 panchayats at intermediate level and 535 panchayats at district level are manned by about 29.2 lakh elected representatives, the broadest representative base that exists in any country.
PRIs empowered to function as institutions of self-government and to prepare plans for economic development and social justice and their empowerment. PRIs constitute the bedrock for the implementation of most of rural development programmes.
Strengthening of Gram Sabha as a vibrant forum of decentralized democracy and effective instrument for ensuring social audit, 1999–2000 observed as the 'Year of Gram Sabha'.
An All India Panchayat Adhyakshas Sammelan was held on 5 and 6 April 2002 to get a feedback from the Adhyakshas in order to revitalize and strengthen PRIs in a time bound manner. In the Sammelan, a 'National Declaration' was adopted by consensus, resolving that state governments would ensure the implementation of the Provisions of Constitution (73rd Amendment) Act, 1992, and Provisions of Panchayats (Extension to Schedules Areas) Act, 1996, in its true spirit by 31 December 2002.

This led to reforming our federal structure and realigning distribution of powers so as to enable grassroots institutions. Such bodies were expected to play an important role especially in the context of globalization. Since the enactment of historic 73rd Constitutional Amendment Act in 1993, PRIs have greatly contributed in shaping the development agenda of our nation by adopting values such as good governance, people's participation, human centred development and accountability (Table 3.2).

Notes

1. Mathew, George, *Panchayati Raj: From Legislation to Movement*, Concept Publishing Company, 2002.

2. Ibid.
3. Majumdar, A.K. and Singh, Bhanwar (eds.), *Historical and Conceptual Development of Panchayati Raj*, New Delhi: Radha Publications, 1997.
4. UNDP, *Decentralization in India: Challenges and Opportunities*, New Delhi, Human Development Resource Centre, 2000, available at http://www.in.undp.org/content/dam/india/docs/decentralisation_india_challenges_opportunities.pdf.
5. Athavale, Pandurang, *Rishismaran*, Sadvichar Darshan Trust, 1999.
6. Mor, Krishna Kumar, *Gram Sabha: Perspectives and Challenges*, Ambala Cantt: The Associated Publishers, 2007.
7. Majumdar, A.K. and Singh, Bhanwar (eds), op. cit.
8. Majumdar, A.K. and Singh Bhanwar (eds), op. cit.
9. Institute of Social Sciences, *Status of Panchayati Raj in the States and Union Territories of India*, New Delhi: Concept Publishing Co., 2000.
10. Goel, S.L. and Shalini, Rajneesh, *Panchayati Raj in India: Theory and Practice*, New Delhi: Deep & Deep Publications, 2003.
11. Ibid.
12. Venkatarangaiah, M. and Pattabhiram, M., *Local Government in India: Select Readings*, New Delhi: Allied Publishers, 1969.
13. The World Bank, *Overview of Rural Decentralization in India*, Vol. III, 2000.
14. Bajpai and Verma, *Panchayati Raj in India: A New Thrust*, Vol. I, 1995.
15. Goel, S.L. and Shalini, Rajneesh, op. cit.
16. Government of India, *Report* of the Team for the Study of Community Projects and National Extension Service (Chairperson: Balwant Rai Mehta), Committee on Plan Projects, National Development Council, New Delhi, November 1957), Vol. I.
17. Kashyap, Anirban, *Panchaytiraj: Views of Founding Fathers and Recommendations of Different Committees*, New Delhi: Lancer Books, 1989.
18. Rai, Manoj, *The State of Panchayats: A Participatory Perspective*, New Delhi: Samskriti, 2001.

19. Government of India, Asoka Mehta Committee, *Report of the Committee on Panchayati Raj Institutions*, Ministry of Agriculture and Irrigation, Department of Rural Development, New Delhi, 1978.
20. Kashyap, Anirban, op. cit.
21. The World Bank, *Overview of Rural Decentralization in India*, Vol. III, 2000.
22. Rai, Manoj, op. cit.
23. Thomas Issac, T.M. and with Franke, Richard, *Local Democracy and Development: People's Campaign for Decentralized Planning in Kerala*, New Delhi: Leftword Books, 2000.
24. Institute of Social Sciences, op. cit.

4

Panchayati Raj in Maharashtra

Maharashtra is situated in the western region of the country. The state shares borders with Gujarat, Madhya Pradesh, Chhattisgarh, Andhra Pradesh, Karnataka, Goa and the UT of Dadra and Nagar Haveli. Maharashtra's gross state domestic product (GSDP) accounted for 12.98 per cent of India's gross domestic product in 2014–2015 – the highest among all states. The GSDP grew at a compound annual growth rate of around 11.1 per cent between 2004–2005 and 2014–2015 to reach US$ 264.8 billion. Total FDI in the state stood at US$ 73.12 billion from April 2000 to May 2015 – again the highest among all states in India. Maharashtra's exports totalled US$ 73.9 billion in 2014–2015. The state's capital, Mumbai, is the commercial capital of India and has evolved into a global financial hub. The city is also home to several global banking and financial service firms. Pune, another major city in the state, has emerged as the educational hub. Thus, Maharashtra today is a key hub for IT, electronics and captive business outsourcing industries. This speaks volumes about the economic and industrial progress the state has made so far.

Maharashtra is the most industrialized state in India and has maintained the leading position in the country. The state is equally a front runner in small-scale industries and boasts of the largest number of special export promotion zones. The state has a well-developed social, physical and industrial infrastructure. Apart from four international and seven domestic airports, the state has two major and fifty-three minor ports. It also has a well-developed power supply grid. Maharashtra's infrastructure sector has grown significantly over the last decade, with a substantial rise in the number of industrial clusters and public-private partnerships.

Although Maharashtra is a highly industrialized state of India, agriculture continues to be the main occupation of the people. Principal crops include rice, jowar, bajra, wheat, pulses, cotton, sugarcane, oil seeds including groundnut, sunflower and soybean, turmeric, onions and other vegetables. The state has large areas, under fruit cultivation of which mangoes, bananas, grapes and famous Nagpur oranges are the main produces. Not only the oranges of Nagpur have earned a name for themselves but the juicy Alphonso mangoes and the grapes being cultivated in Nashik and other regions of the state have become well known and earn considerable foreign exchange as well. Irrigation facilities are being extended so that agriculture could be made less dependent on rain water.

Local Governance in Maharashtra

Maharashtra has been a leading and pioneering state so far as implementing any scheme of decentralization in India is concerned. In fact, village panchayats in Maharashtra had traditionally functioned as the main centre of administration (ISS, 2000: 184). Before independence many acts were passed by British which contributed to the development of local self-government institutions in Maharashtra, for example, the Bombay Local Fund Act of 1869, the Bombay

Local Boards Act of 1923, the Bombay Village Panchayat Act of 1920, Hatch Committee was also appointed in 1925 (ISS, 2000: 185). After the reorganization of states in 1956, a comprehensive legislation for village panchayats called the Bombay Village Panchayat Act, 1958, was passed. This act, as amended from time to time, remains in force to this day (ISS, 2000: 186).

On 1 May 1960, the present state of Maharashtra was formed, with Bombay (renamed as Mumbai in 1995) as its capital. Although the report of the Balwant Rai Mehta study team had been made public, the state government preferred to appoint a Committee on Democratic Decentralization headed by Vasantrao Naik to study the subject of Panchayati Raj in all its aspects and to make a model proposal for the state (Figure 4.1). It was on the basis of the recommendations of the Naik Committee that a comprehensive legislation, the Maharashtra Zilla Parishads and Panchayat Samitis Act, 1961, was enacted and Zilla Parishads and Panchayat Samitis were constituted in May 1962 (ISS, 2000).

The objective of the act was to provide for establishment in rural areas, Zilla Parishads and Panchayat Samitis, to assign to them local government functions and also entrust the execution of certain works and development schemes of the state five-year plans to such bodies, and to provide for the decentralization of powers and functions under certain enactment to these local bodies for the purpose of promoting development of democratic institutions and securing greater measure of participation by the people in the State Plan and in local government affairs.

Organization of Rural Local Governance in Maharashtra

Zilla Parishad

Zilla Parishad functions at the district level. It looks after the administration of the rural areas of the district and its office is located at the district headquarters. There are 33 Zilla Parishads in Maharashtra, one each in every district, as shown below in Table 4.1.

Table 4.1

Number of Elected Representatives in Zilla Parishads

	General	*SCs*	*STs*	*Women*	*Total*
Total	1,502	215	234	653	1,951
Percentage	76.98	11.01	11.99	33.47	100.00

Source: Maharashtra Profile, https://www.scribd.com/document/94696005/15Maharashtraprofile.

Panchayat Samiti

Panchayat Samiti works for the villages of the tehsil or taluka that together are called a development block. It is the link between the Gram Panchayat and Zilla Parishad. There are 355 Panchayat Samitis in Maharashtra as shown in Table 4.2.

Table 4.2

Number of Elected Representatives in Panchayat Samitis

	General	*SC*	*ST*	*Women*	*Total*
Total	3,005	429	468	1,317	3,902
Percentage	77.01	10.99	11.99	33.75	100.00

Source: Maharashtra Profile, https://www.scribd.com/document/94696005/ 15Maharashtraprofile.

Gram Panchayat

Gram Panchayat functions at the village level. It is the foundation of the panchayat system. A Gram Panchayat can be set up in villages with a population of more than 500. There can be a common Gram Panchayat for two or more villages if the population of the villages is less than 500. There are 28,813 Gram Panchayats in Maharashtra as shown in Table 4.3.

Table 4.3

Number of Elected Representatives in Gram Panchayats

	General	*SCs*	*STs*	*Women*	*Total*
Total	1,72,370	24,624	26,863	75,148	2,23,857
Percentage	77.0	10.99	12.00	33.56	100.00

Source: Maharashtra Profile, https://www.scribd.com/document/94696005/15Maharashtraprofile.

Gram Panchayats in Maharashtra

As stated above, Gram Panchayat is the foundation of the Panchayati Raj system. Members of the Gram Panchayat are elected directly by the village people on the basis of adult franchise by the Gram Sabha, which comprises the adult mass of the village, for a term of five years. A candidate contesting in this election must be 21 years old. The minimum number of members elected is seven and the maximum is seventeen. The Sarpanch or chairperson is the head of the Gram Panchayat. The elected members of the Gram Panchayat elect from among themselves a Sarpanch and a Deputy Sarpanch for a term of five years. In some places, the Sarpanch is directly elected by village people. The Sarpanch presides over the meetings of the Gram Panchayat and also supervises its working. He implements the development schemes of the village. The Deputy Sarpanch, who has the power to make his own decisions, assists the Sarpanch in his work.

Financial Powers of Gram Panchayats

Gram Panchayats have been authorized to accord administrative approval and sanction expenditure for the work costing up to ₹ 3 lakh for which technical sanction of Junior Engineer is required. If the cost of work is more than ₹ 3 lakh and up to ₹ 10 lakh, administrative approval of Panchayat Samiti and technical sanction of Assistant Engineer is essential. In the case of work costing more than ₹ 10 lakh, administrative approval of Zilla Parishad and technical sanction of Executive Engineer is essential. With the passage of 73rd Amendment, India sought to grant autonomy to the institutions of local self-governments. But the close scrutiny of the state legislations reveals the fact that local government institutions are not yet freed from the clutches of the bureaucracy. During the field work conducted in the villages of Thane district, the Gram Sevaks, Sarpanchas and villagers complained regarding this. According to the Section 124 of the Bombay Village Panchayats Act, 1958, Gram Panchayats can levy taxes on buildings and land, shops, hotels, trade, fairs, festivals, fee for supply of water from wells and tanks and piped water supply, grazing cattle and car and tonga stands.

Gram Sabha

Gram Sabhas have been given extensive powers under Section 7 of the Mumbai Village Panchayats Act, 1958, as amended in 2003. Six meetings of the Gram Sabha have been provided for every year. It is mandatory to call the meeting of the women members of the Gram Sabha before every regular meeting of the Gram Sabha. A panchayat is required to obtain permission of the Gram Sabha for incurring any expenditure on the development. Gram Sabha is also competent to approve the social or economic development plan and projects to be implemented by the panchayat. Gram Sabha has also the power to select beneficiaries for individual beneficiary schemes of the state/central government. Unless exempted by the Gram Sabha, all the government, semi-government and panchayat employees are required to attend the meetings of the Gram Sabha. The most empowering decision of the state of Maharashtra has been reserving 50 per cent seats for women in Gram Panchayats. This has definitely bolstered the confidence of rural women across Maharashtra. Civil society organizations such as

Mahila Rajsatta Andolan have welcomed this decision of the government. A special Gram Sabha for women in the villages is also being organized on a regular basis in the state since 2003. The issues discussed in Mahila Gram Sabha must be discussed and considered in the regular Gram Sabha. It is mandatory for the Sarpanch to present before the regular Gram Sabha the proceedings of the Mahila Gram Sabha. Subjects such as child sex ratio, anti-liquor campaign, nutrition, drinking water, sanitation, public distribution system, women and child development are generally discussed in these Mahila Gram Sabhas.

The Gram Sabha has disciplinary control over the government, semi-government and panchayat employees working in the village including the matters relating to their daily attendance in the office. It is provided that the Gram Sabha shall report to the concerned BDO the irregularities, if any, committed by any of such employees. The BDO shall consider such report within the period of three months from the date of its receipt. Such matters and the actions taken thereon shall be reviewed in the regular meetings of the Panchayat Samiti. If the BDO fails to dispose off such reports within the specified period of three months, the same shall, on the expiry of the said period, stand transferred to the Chief Executive Officer of the concerned Zilla Parishad for disposal, whose decision shall be final. The Chief Executive Officer of the Zilla Parishad shall take the decision on such reports so transferred to him, within a period of three months from the date of their receipt. Minimum 15 per cent of the total members of the Gram Sabha or a total of 100 persons whichever is less shall constitute a quorum for the meeting of Gram Sabha.

The state of Maharashtra, along with states such as Kerala, Karnataka and West Bengal, has been consistently maintaining a good devolution index. Devolution index, which is developed by ministry of Panchayati Raj, ranks the

Map 4.1

Thane District

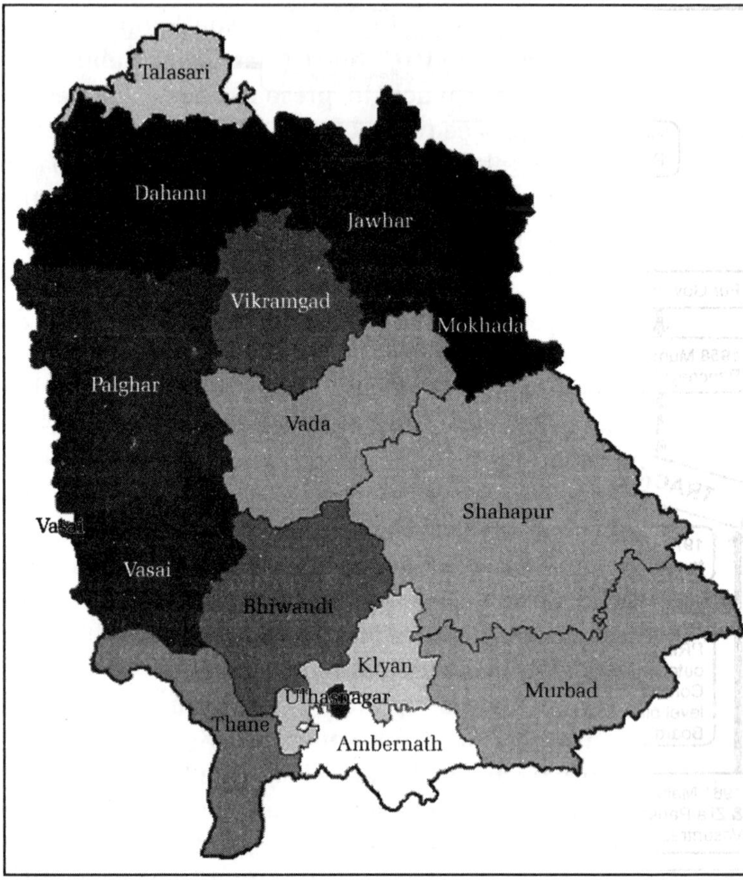

Source: Google Images.

Figure 4.1

Tracking the History of Panchayati Raj in Maharashtra

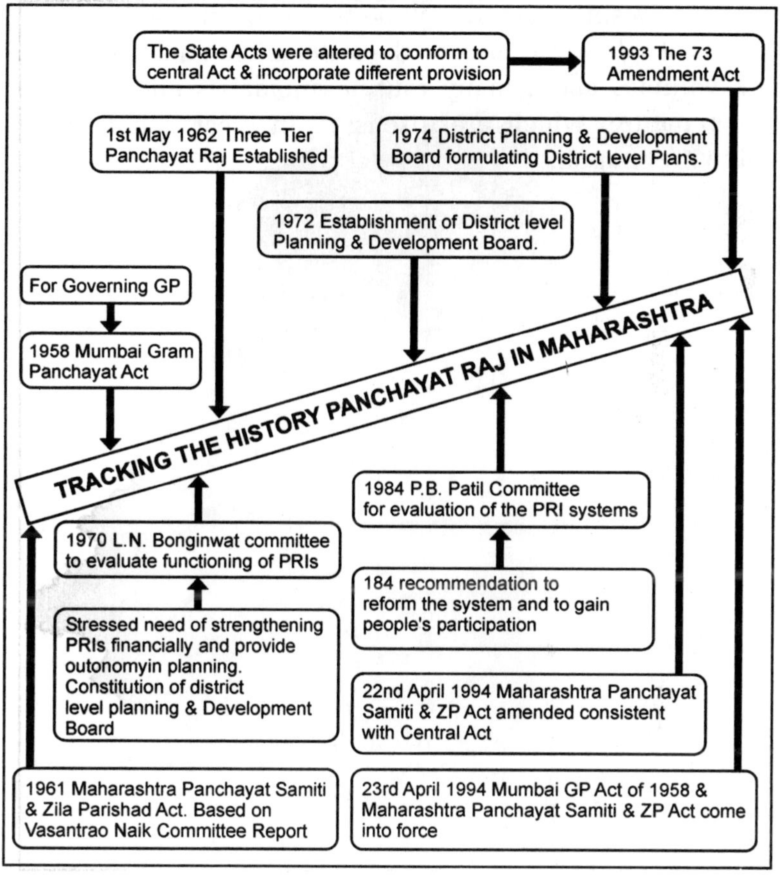

Source: Rural Maharashtra: A Saga of Development, Government of Maharashtra.

states depending on the enabling environment created in the respective states. It takes into consideration three important criteria such as devolution of functions, functionaries and finances. Despite overall high performance in enabling institutions of self-governance in the state, micro analysis of PRIs talk volumes about many routine anomalies and dysfunctional nature, which are discussed in great detail in the following chapter.

5

Practising Local Governance

Some Issues

The swelling inflation rate, the uprising of youth in Kashmir for an autonomous state within a nation-sate, the neglected tribals and weaker sections of the society turning into Maoists or Naxalites are the few examples compelling us to reflect upon the traditional paradigms of governance. The 'excluded' needs to be 'included'. The national and local have to work together in the global context that controls the polity and economy to a great extent. The post-Washington consensus crafted by Joseph Stiglitz[1] gives a call to government to focus on economic policies, basic education, health, roads, law and order and environmental protection. Thus, the state is not expected to crunch in size and function, rather it is expected to work in tandem with market forces and work in a complementary manner. The government is incarnated today in the form of governance model. The trajectory of governance today not only focuses on the institutions of the state at the centre but also tries to give an equal space to the units of local governance. The term *local governance* plays a significant role in shaping the tone and tenor of the schemes of development at the grassroots level.

In *India: Development and Participation* (2002), Jean Dreze and Amartya Sen talk about the lag that exists between the democratic ideals, democratic institutions and democratic practices. The performance of the democratic institutions is contingent on a wide range of social, economic, educational and political conditions. In the context of such deep compromises which define our polity and society today, it will be interesting to understand the practice of PRIs in the country and also the process rather than the prescriptions given in the Constitutional Amendment Act of 1993. There was also an attempt made to examine the working of these institutions in the context of a macro phenomenon called 'globalization'. The PRIs may appear to be too insignificant to the world economy but these micro institutions do contribute to the national development and are affected by the policies made at the central level. And, governments across the globe can no more remain unaffected by the macro process of globalization. So, in a three-tier and complex federal polity like India, forces of globalization are overtly or covertly going to have an impact on the grassroots organizations. Therefore, this study aims to generate insights, gleaned from close observation of the villages in an area that is usually discussed in terms of institutions and policy making. This is done in the backdrop of the fact that villages did not remain unaffected with the onset of globalization in India. Economic opportunities, growth of markets and spread of information technology have changed rural India.

This chapter draws conclusions from the field studies conducted and suggest the future course of action to craft revitalized PRIs. To collect the first-hand information of the ground-level realities and understand the modalities of the grassroots governance, the state of Maharashtra was selected. The reason being was its high performance in comparison to many other states on a variety of development indicators.

There are total 33 districts in the state of Maharashtra, out of which Thane district was purposely chosen for being one of the most urbanized districts and also for experiencing multiple effects of globalization. Three talukas (blocks), namely, Shahpur, Murbad and Kalyan were shortlisted (see Map 5.1). These talukas are closer to urbanized and globalized city of Mumbai. Impressions of effects of globalization in certain aspects of village life were closely observed. For example, availability of foreign brand of cola water bottles, the World Bank funding directly to few panchayats, availability of the information and communication technology (wireless land line and mobile phones), trade of agricultural and other produces happening at the taluka headquarters, market orientation and so on. To understand the life of these villages from the perspective of operation of local governance system in the context of globalization, a few indicators of development and indices of democratic participation were picked up to draw conclusions.

Field Observations

During the study, a host of important issues such as electoral process and practices, state of education in the villages, functioning of Gram Sabha, people's empowerment and deepening of democratic values were studied since they are an important gateway to examine their performance as institutions of self-governance. Despite the fragmented social set-up, elite capture and control of the Gram Panchayat, state interference in the functioning of the institutions of local self-governance, poor participation of common people in the affairs of the Gram Panchayat and weak representation and pitiable participation of women leaders and members in these institutions, PRIs have been instrumental to advance humanitarian values, percolation of ideas of equality and has been able to building a strong community life.

Co-relation between the State of Education and Distance from an Urban Centre

Education elevates and encourages even the modest and humblest of the human being coming from any strata of the society. Indian villages for large number of years even after independence were devoid of the opportunities for their educational development. An urban-centric approach of the government created sharp divisions as far as availability of opportunities for educational growth were concerned, especially in the countryside. One thing which attracted the attention was the co-relation between the proximity of the village to a city or an urbanized area and the level of literacy or education. The nearer a city, the greater is the level of literacy in a village. So, the literacy rate in Kalbhunde, a village in Shahpur block, was lowest, at 40 per cent, and that in Gotheghar, a village in Kalyan-Dombivali block, was highest, at 95 per cent (see Table 5.1). One needs to understand that not only the level of education but also the availability of many other basic amenities has a co-relation with the distance of the village from an urban area.

Table 5.1

Literacy Rate in Selected Villages

Name of the Village Panchayat	*Name of the Taluka*	*Literacy Rate (%)*	*Distance from Closest Town*
Azade Gao	Kalyan	80	3 km from Dombivali
Katai Gao	Kalyan	80	5 km from Dombivali
Ambele Budruk	Murbad	80	8 km from Murbad
Khandpe	Murbad	80	12 km from Murbad
Wafe	Shahpur	90	4 km from Asangaon
Kalbhunde	Shahpur	35 to 40	57 km from Asangaon
Gotheghar	Shahpur	95	3 km From Asangaon

Source: Gram Sevak of the concerned villages, and Gram Panchayat records.

It is fruitful to contextualize the spatial dimension while looking at the villages, the latter are changing rapidly because of the globalization-induced changes. It is pertinent to note here that only 14.28 per cent of the villages have colleges or secondary schools (see Tables 5.2 and 5.3). Except Azade Gao village (see Table 5.3), no village has a higher secondary school. Azade Gao has many schools and colleges simply because, first, it lies within the Maharashtra Industrial Development Corporation area, and, second, this Gram Panchayat was previously under the control of Kalyan-Dombivali Municipal Corporation and was virtually a semi-urban area. The village is very close to the city of Dombivali, which is buzzing with the effects of urbanization, modernization and globalization.

Table 5.2

Educational Facilities in Selected Villages

Name of the Village Panchayat	*Anganwadi (Day Care Centre)*	*No. of Schools*
Azade Gao	1	Many schools and colleges
Katai Gao	1	1 up to 7th grade
Ambele Budruk	1	1
Khandpe	1	1
Wafe	3	2 Zilla Parishad (ZP) schools up to 7th grade
Kalbhunde	2	3 primary schools
Gotheghar	4	3 ZP schools

Source: Gram Sevak of the concerned villages, and Gram Panchayat records.

Table 5.3

Educational Facility in Selected Villages (in Percentile)

Educational Facility	*Percentage*
Anganwadi	100
Primary Schools	100
Secondary Schools	14.28
College	14.28

Source: Gram Sevak of the concerned villages, and Gram Panchayat records.

Local Democracy at Work

The electoral practices that prevail at the local level are an important indicator of the practice of local governance at the grassroots level. Table 5.4 brings to our notice that the spirit of democracy in the villages surveyed is very high. People do exhibit a great sense of enthusiasm as far as praxis of direct democracy is concerned. They are excited to participate and vote. Katai village stands out, with its 100 per cent voting turnout, followed by Wafe and Gotheghar with 95 per cent voting turnout. However, conclusions drawn from merely the percentage of voting may be deceptive. The details of the methods and mode of elections adopted reveal that the dream of a true local democracy is yet unfulfilled. A cursory glance at Figure 5.1 testifies to this fact. In 28.57 per cent of the villages, members of the Gram Panchayat are elected unopposed, 57.14 per cent villages conducted elections in accordance with the due process of the law and 14.28 per cent of the villages opted for both types of election. Globalization and a concurrent process of urbanization, which indirectly affect the village

Figure 5.1

How Elections are Conducted?

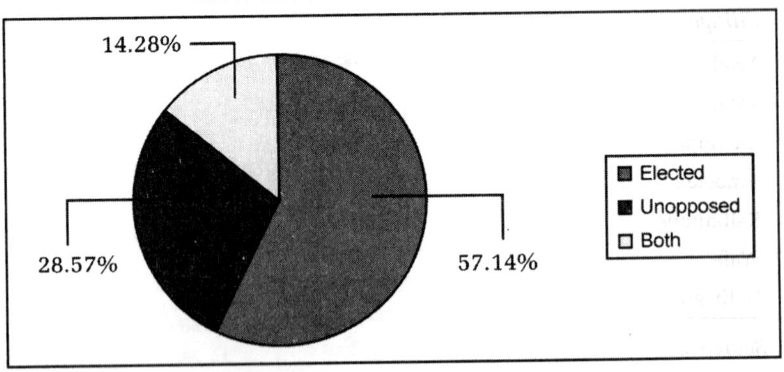

Source: Gram Sevak of the concerned villages, and Gram Panchayat records.

life, have not been able to change the social stratification in village societies in any major way. In reality castes have been entrenched and continue to influence and dominate the village politics. (See Table 5.5 for caste wise demographic profile of the surveyed villages.) Caste system is explicitly discriminatory system of laws, which is against both the modern notions of liberty and equality. It has no sense of fraternity, except within the caste group. The phenomenon of class is also emerging in these villages on account of the economic disparities created because of disproportionate land distribution and progressive land acquisitions taking place by the government. (See Table 5.6 for poverty profile of the surveyed villages). These things have sharpened the divisions in the village societies and are fuelled by factitious party politics taking shape at the grass-roots level. Villages are still in the grip of either the dominant castes or elites of the highly stratified village societies. Political parties are successful in dividing the village vote bank and elections are conveniently avoided in the name of consensual elections.

Table 5.4

Awareness about Gram Panchayat Elections

Name of the Village	*Percentage of Voting in Last Election*	*How it was Conducted*
Azade	60	Some unopposed and some elected
Katai	100	All elected
Khandpe	55	Unopposed
Ambele Budruk	50	Unopposed
Kalbhunde	80	Elected
Wafe	95	Elected
Gotheghar	95	Elected

Source: Gram Sevak of the concerned villages, and Gram Panchayat records.

Table 5.5

Demography of the Selected Villages

Name of Village Panchayat	*Male Population*	*Female Population*	*SCs*	*STs*	*Total Population*
Azade	NA	NA	NA	NA	13,758
Katai	NA	NA	NA	NA	18,056
Ambele Budruk	543	466	121	49	1,009
Khandpe	497	471	189	27	968
Wafe	1,430	1,414	222	606	2,844
Kalbhunde	427	464	–	891	891 100% ST Population
Gotheghar	1,886	1,711	243	256	4,096

Source: Gram Sevak of the concerned villages, and Gram Panchayat records.

Table 5.6

Percentage of Poverty

Name of the Village Panchayat	*Total No. of Families*	*BPL Families*	*% of Poverty*
Azade	3,769	71	1.88
Katai	297	20	6.73
Ambele Budruk	176	38	21.5
Khandpe	188	34 approx.	18.08
Wafe	464	78	16.81
Kalbhunde	195	163	83.58
Gotheghar	934	195	20.87

Source: Gram Sevak of the concerned villages, and Gram Panchayat records.

Similar observations have been cited by Girish Kumar (2006) in his extensive work on local democracy in India. Kumar's field observations reveal that elections are held merely for the sake of form. They call it a unanimous election or consensus selection of leaders. Kumar highlights the issue that merely holding elections in accordance with the relevant procedure actually does not serve any purpose of local democracy. He also observes that elections do not necessarily mean horizontal dispersal of power or deepening of democracy. In a vast and diversified country like India, decentralization of powers and functions to meet global challenges and to achieve goals, sustainable development becomes essential. For this to happen, elections must actually take place, rather than merely be paid lip-service. In an interview, Kumar said that each village has four sets of people as under:

1. Ruling elites are those who are in command of the village panchayat. It is necessary to examine whether these elites are elected or selected according to custom. Are they really promoting street-level democracy? After visiting many villages across India, Kumar (2006) concluded that Indian PRIs are promoting 'illiberal democracy'. The controlling elites are generally corrupt, monopolized and patronized.

2. The second set of people is those who are in opposition to the elites. They are the mirror image of the ruling elites: those who are waiting to take their place. They are the elites in-waiting.

3. The next set of people is those who are the powerless, that is, those who live below the poverty line. They are the asset-less, semi-literate or illiterate people, especially from lower social castes such as SCs or STs (social groups at the lowest rungs of social hierarchy).

4. A very few people in villages have a different mental make-up, are courageous and can think beyond their own self-interest and can raise issues and questions.

Although decentralization ensures a deepening of democracy, it sometimes may lead to the creation of democratic elites. The dominant caste or ethnic groups often tend to command or dominate the village power structure. For this reason, Dr Ambedkar (the architect of the Indian

Constitution) was also severely critical of the idea of 'Gram Swaraj' (local self-governance). However, let us try to look at such local self-governance as a practice intended to enrich the experiment and experience of democracy. As John Stuart Mill has stated, 'A people may be unprepared for good institutions; but to kindle a desire for them is a necessary part of the preparation'. This very practice of local self-governance is conceived out of the cherished dream of our father of the nation that one day villages will be self-managed and self-sufficient. Our national elections to the Lok Sabha (the lower house of the Indian Parliament) have endured and stood the test of the time and have shown marvellous resilience. Even the changing composition of the national parliament has revealed a shift from educated elites in the formative years of the nation to today when a huge chunk of Members of Parliament come from different socio-cultural and agricultural backgrounds. The parliament today represents a good mix of urban and rural populations representing the *Bharat* and India. It will take time to deepen the practice of free and fair elections at the grassroots level. The present state of electoral practices in these villages is proof enough of the lag that exists between democratic ideals and democratic practices. The understanding of politics and change in rural India is critically linked to an understanding of power and the oppressive structures of domination that characterize peasant society (Singh and Sharma, 2007).

However, taking a different line, one can say that these elections – no matter how they are conducted – are one way of seeking legitimacy at the grassroots level. The very concept of the desire to secure legitimacy at the grassroots level is a fresh one and is to be greatly appreciated in a caste- and class-ridden society like India. By closely observing the villages, it was discovered that with the rise of media, especially after the onslaught of globalization and information and communication technology, people from a cross-section of the village society have shown a keen interest in coming to the forefront, to be brave and bold and to find out about what is happening in the Gram Panchayat and what is being done by the Gram Panchayat. An interesting observation made during the study was that of Kalbhunde village which unanimously boycotted the Lok Sabha elections and only 32 persons in village voted. There was 74 per cent participation in the same village in elections to the Vidhan Sabha (the lower house of the state legislature in India); and greater participation (100%) in the Gram Panchayat elections. They objected it because for the past ten years, they have not had electricity in the village or good roads. In people's opinions, the leaders who were selected as Members of Parliament or elected to the state legislative assembly were not representative of the local area. Thus, the constitutionally mandated election taking place at regular intervals to units of local self-governance is a major tool in the hands of people at the grassroots level to express displeasure and disapproval.

Transparency in Government: The Right to Information

The governance discourse focus on attributes such as accountability, transparency, people's participation and development that is centred on people's choices. This seems to be unachievable in the absence of a well-designed Right to Information (RTI) Act. It ensures empowerment of people and also places them in position of control over the political process. Merely establishing institutions at the grassroots through constitutional mechanisms do not guarantee its successful functioning. In fact, many a time, institutions underperform or become dysfunctional in the long run in the absence of a vibrant oversight mechanism in place. Since 2005, an RTI Act has been in operation across the length and breadth of India. This has been done with a clear objective to realize the dream of a participatory democracy. It plays a quintessential role when we contextualize its role with regard to grassroots democracy. People in the villages can enforce the Gram Panchayat to secure their entitlements and benefits given to them through a plethora of centrally funded schemes and state-funded programmes. It also helps generate confidence of people in the government. According to the 2005 Act, panchayats are required to appoint Public Information Officer to receive and handle requests for information. Provision of information has been made a constitutional obligation for panchayats under the new legal regime in place. Many states such as Uttarakand, Rajasthan and Chhattisgarh have tried to implement the same in their own states.

This act was passed by the parliament after long battle fought by civil society organizations coming from the grassroots. These organizations have been instrumental in empowering people at the bottom of socio-economic and political hierarchy. The RTI Act is an important tool of maintaining accountability and control over the legislative statesmen at all levels, the political as well as permanent executives and government in general. While surveying the villages, the Gram Sevak of each village communicated unanimously that he receives a number of applications along with a large number of questions from villagers each day. However, after carefully cross-checking and assessing the Gram Panchayat records, it was realized that either there are none or very few registered applications for seeking information under the RTI Act. One Gram Sevak very proudly stated that in his village no applications had been registered in the past two to three years under the said act. He told that he provides people with information when they approach him or shows them Gram Panchayat records directly. This is in a sense quite true as he agreed to show the researcher the same records when he was approached at the village office to provide the information. However, the basic issue is that in the absence of any training about how to use the RTI Act, the whole purpose of accountability and control gets marred. The practice of social audits remains a distant dream to be fulfilled in the selected villages in Thane district.

Founding Stone: Gram Sabha

The Gram Sabha is the cornerstone of the entire design of democratic decentralization in India initiated through the 73rd Amendment to the Constitution. The Gram Sabha serves as the foundation of the PRIs. It is a forum comprising each and every registered voter on the electoral roll of the village. Gram Sabha enables village people to discuss and debate the issues that concern their lives immediately as well as remotely. The most significant aspect of this novel experiment in the village politics is that these Gram Sabhas have been crafted into constitutional bodies. The Gram Sabha is expected to regularly meet and debate on a host of issues. In a way, it is visualized to be a miniature of the parliamentary democracy. However, the people's participation in the activities of Gram Sabha brings lot of despair and demotivation to our minds.

Constitutionally, the Gram Panchayats are to be managed by elected representatives and Gram Sabha is to be attended by all the registered voters on the electoral roll of a village. An instant look at Table 5.7 shows that the dream of a direct democracy through the medium of the Gram Sabha is still far from being achieved. Only two villages, Azade Gao and Kalbhunde, stand out as far as attendance in Gram Sabha is concerned, with 70 per cent and 80 per cent attendance respectively. Other villages are actually struggling to inspire people to attend the Gram Sabha meetings, with a meagre 20 per cent attendance in Khandpe village (the lowest of all the villages). And, one becomes more concerned when we understand the fact that mere attendance does not reflect real participation of people in village governance. There are few questions which need to be answered. Who gets a chance to ask questions? Who actually asks questions? How many questions are asked? How many of these questions are actually answered? Which questions are conveniently prevented from coming to the floor of the Gram Sabha meetings? Is Gram Sabha becoming merely an agency of the state or central government? Is it only a body to select beneficiaries and sites of construction for centrally sponsored schemes and programmes? We come to some bewildering conclusions. Most of the time, Gram Sabha meetings are adjourned on account of lack of quorum, that is, minimum attendance required to conduct a meeting. On the contrary, we came across a Gram Panchayat called Azade Gao where if a Gram Sabha meeting is called, a big pandal has to be set up to conduct the proceedings. Looking into the reasons for this, it was found that this Gram Panchayat came under the jurisdiction of the Maharashtra Industrial Development Corporation as well. Most of the village dwellers are educated government servants. Highly aware and politically active people reside in this village. When Gram Sabha is called, the overwhelming attendance compels the panchayat to set up a pandal to conduct the meeting. People of this village regularly come to meetings with their problems and complaints, thus keeping the members of the Gram Panchayat on their toes. In recently concluded panchayat election of 2015 in the state of Maharashtra, this Gram Panchayat was converted into a Nagar Palika in the midst of lot of resistance from the villagers though. The functioning of the Gram Sabha was closely followed in Wafe village as well. It was easy to deduce that this Gram Panchayat is quiet active and participative. The attendance in the Gram Sabha is comparatively better than other villages. The common people approach the Sarpanch and Gram Sevak with their problems and try to get it redressed using innumerable state and central government sponsored schemes.

Table 5.7

Attendance in the Gram Sabha Meetings

Name of the Village Panchayat	*Percentage*	*Quorum (Minimum Attendance)*
Azade Gao	70	Most of the time
Katai Gao	30	Rarely
Ambele Budruk	30	Rarely
Khandpe	20	Rarely
Wafe	40	Rarely
Kalbhunde	80	Most of the time
Gotheghar	50	Rarely

Source: Gram Sevak of the concerned villages, and Gram Panchayat records.

The vibrancy and efficacy of Gram Sabha will remain dismal if it does not exercise its capacity and authority to perform its constitutionally assigned roles and responsibilities. Low participation in Gram Sabha meetings and irregular and informal ways of its conduct are some of the major concerns at the grassroots. These can be attributed to factors such as deeply rooted caste divide in villages, subordination of women in village societies and influence of the dominant castes in the villages. However, one cannot neglect the fact with the waves of change under globalization and a concomitant process of urbanization, villages are experiencing what is called as 'rurbanization'. The village society is now changing for the better. While maintaining the ethos and flavour of the village life, modern outlooks and ideas are fundamentally shaking the entrenched caste system. Gram Sabha is now seen as a powerful medium by the lower castes to voice their choices. This has definitely leveraged their confidence and given them platform to articulate their needs and demands. In the present study, the constructive role played by the Gram Sabha after the implementation of the Constitutional Amendment Act of 1993 is highlighted.

The Gram Sabha (forum of discussion where all the voters can participate) plays a dominant role in deciding various matters. Developmental proposals are presented in Gram Sabha meetings and these are discussed and then, after the approval of the Gram Sabha, they are forwarded to the department concerned at either block or district level. This sometimes obstructs the Gram Sabha's freedom to perform constitutionally guaranteed functions. Although proposals are prepared and passed by the Gram Sabha, their implementation must receive a green signal from the block or district level departments. The finance required for micro or macro projects must be approved by departmental heads. The Gram Panchayat is not capable of raising money to a great extent. Thus, in practice the appointed bureaucracy which sits over the heads of Gram Panchayat undermines the whole spirit of the decisions taken by a popularly elected body.

In the Gram Sabha meeting of Gotheghar village, the agenda of the Gram Sabha was to decide the claims for granting of forest rights under STs and Other Traditional Forest Dwellers (Recognition of Forest Rights) Act, 2005. As per the Act, Gram Sabha is responsible for determining the nature and extent of forest rights given to the people of this village and prepare a list of beneficiaries (claimants) and pass a resolution on those claims granting them forest rights. This Gram Sabha meeting was third meeting in a row on this issue. In this meeting, all came with their file of official documents, and the Sabha was supposed to check its validity and pass it to the next stage. Around 40 people attended this Sabha, including a large number of women. Three to four of them had formal education. Some of them knew how to read and write. Half of them were illiterate. All present were from STs. One of the women, who seemed to be a leader of these women, explained the benefits of this act and had organized them to come to Gram Sabha and avail the benefits of the act.

Very few of them clearly knew for what purpose they had come to the Gram Sabha meeting. The meeting was headed by the Sarpanch. But, the woman Sarpanch did not say a single word. She was sitting silently and was an inactive participant of the meeting. She left the meeting half way. The meeting was conducted by the Gram Sevak who is appointed by the Panchayat Samiti to help in the functioning of Gram Panchayat. This Gram Sevak was doing his job well explaining the details of the act. Some of the residents of this village took active interest and participated in the proceedings and were playing the role of self-appointed leaders. This ultimately helps the villagers. Each claimant's file was checked in front of the Sabha and was then approved by the Sabha. However, most of them were interested in their own claim. They had little knowledge of the details of the issue. Few of the members did raise questions on the claims forwarded by some people to just cross check but later they were settled by way of discussion. The Gram Sevak was of the opinion that the PRIs are benefiting the people and as per the 73rd Amendment Act, the Gram Sabha was a tool of empowering people, giving them a platform to voice their demands. But, many a time, the party politics kills the whole idea of democratic governance at the grassroots level. A woman, who was content with the developmental work done in their village, said that they do regularly attend the Gram Sabha meetings and use this forum to express their opinion. But even they are divided into camps as they belong to one or the other political party. This actually hampers the activities of the Gram Sabha. What is needed at this juncture is more of a functional autonomy accompanied by fiscal autonomy. It is only then the Panchayati Raj system can become successful and can be hailed as a genuine institution of local self-governance.

While observing the proceedings of a Gram Sabha meeting in Katai, it was found that the male members decide the discourse of the meetings held. Women members were just nodding their heads. However, later, it was discovered that female members put up their issues indirectly through the Gram Sevika. As per the amended Maharashtra Village Panchayat Act, there is provision of 50 per cent reservation for women in all three tiers of PRIs in Maharashtra. In addition, women have been given 50 per cent reservation in the district planning committees as well. This ensures their participation not only in policy and decision-making process but also in the project planning and implementation process. It also brings fresh perspectives to the whole agenda of development at grassroots level. For instance, one Gram Sabha of Katai village created an agenda to generate awareness for the Sampoorna Swachhata Abhiyan. Importance of using toilets was explained in detail and also explained how to keep the vicinity clean and hygienic.

Since 2003, the state of Maharashtra has been conducting an exclusive Mahila Gram Sabha for the women members of every village. In such a Gram Sabha in Katai village, all women were told about the importance of water purification. They were also given a bottle of Aquaclore to purify home water. Most of the women from this village attend the Gram Sabha meetings. They come to meetings with their problems and try to solve them. The women of this village are quiet active through Mahila Bachat Gat (Table 5.8). They are also aware of various bank activities now. They participate in the developmental activities of the village. In this village, a novel idea of 'Haldi Kumkum Milan' (traditional festival of Maharashtra) was executed in which soap boxes were distributed to village women as a return gift (*Van* in Marathi). The idea behind this was to explain them the importance of washing hands after using toilet.

Table 5.8

Level of Participation of Women in Mahila Bachat Gat (Women's Savings Groups)

Name of Village Panchayat	*Mahila Bachat Gat*	*Female Population*	*Percentage*
Azade Gao	3	NA	–
Katai Gao	4	NA	–
Ambele Budruk	5 Below Poverty Line (BPL) =3	466	17.17
Khandpe	4 BPL=2	471	12.74
Wafe	13	1,414	9.19
Kalbhunde	5	464	10.78
Gotheghar	12	1,711	7.01

Source: Gram Sevak of the concerned villages, and Gram Panchayat records.

In two Gram Sabha meetings in Kandpe village, an abysmally low attendance was found. The Gram Sevika said that the agenda of this meeting had no attractive scheme and people were busy in canvassing for the forthcoming Vidhan Sabha elections. But the positive aspect of this participatory democracy is as Dreze and Sen (2002) highlighted that it ensures discussions, debates and meaningful exchange of views. This is essential to the formation of values and social and economic priorities.

The grassroots governance has tremendous potential to advance and be an instrument in the process of village development. The only requirement is to tap the local energies and innovative ideas of the village folks and try to incorporate them into the ambit of local self-governance. The Constitution of India opens with following words: 'We the people of India', which reflect the spirit of our polity and democracy. The Constitution envisages a sovereign nation where each one enjoys liberty, equality and justice and is bound with each other with a sense of brotherhood. Mere declaration of these ideals does not create a nation of our dreams. They are to be taught and learned through formal and informal institutions. The PRIs serve as a learning ground of producing responsible citizens and responsive leaders of tomorrow. In the last chapter, we will discuss how to revitalize the PRI system in the present context.

Availability of Basic Services

In the villages surveyed in Thane district, one outstanding and remarkable observation was that road facilities were impressive (barring a few exceptions). Water is a matter of concern in all these villages. Some villages have excellent water provision schemes. A few villages also have been successful in obtaining the World Bank grants for providing water through pipelines. A total of 85.71 per cent of villages have good roads and water facilities (see Table 5.9). As shown in the table, all the villages except Kalbhunde have water provision through a pipeline. Primary health centres (PHCs) are available in the block headquarters near to the villages (see Table 5.10). Similarly, 57.14 per cent have access to good PHCs (see Table 5.9). On the sanitation front, these villages also fare well. Again, 57.14 per cent of the

Table 5.9

Quality of the Basic Services

Public Service	*Good*	*Average*	*Poor*
Water	85.71% 6/7	14.28% 1/7	–
Roads	85.71% 6/7	–	14.28% 1/7
PHC	57.14% 4/7	28.57% 2/7	14.28% 1/7
Toilets	57.14% 4/7	42.85% 3/7	–
Schools	42.85% 3/7	28.57% 2/7	28.57% 2/7

Source: Gram Sevak of the concerned villages, and Gram Panchayat records.

Table 5.10

Record of Availability of Public Services

Name of the Village Panchayat	*Toilets*	*Availability of Roads*	*No. of Schools*	*PHC*	*Availability of Water*
Azade Gao	4 public toilets	100% pukka (concrete) roads	Many schools and colleges	At Shivale	Pipeline available
Katai Gao	4 public toilets	100% pukka roads	1upto 7th grade	At Nilaje	Pipeline available
Ambele Budruk	7 public toilets	100% pukka roads	1	Not available	Well or bore well few have tap water
Khandpe	Public toilets	100% pukka roads	1	Not available	Khandpe dam
Wafe	5 public toilets and 339 private	100% pukka roads	2 ZP schools up to 7th grade	At Shahpur	Pipeline available
Kalbhunde	Public and personal	No roads. Only kuchha (non-concrete) roads	3 primary schools	At Kasara	Poor availability
Gotheghar	10 public toilets	100% pukka roads	3 ZP schools	At Shahpur	Pipeline available

Source: Gram Sevak of the concerned villages, and Gram Panchayat records.

villages have good sanitation facilities. A quick glance at Table 5.10 reveals the number of public and private toilets available in these villages. Wafe stands out with 339 personal toilets.

Note

1. Joseph Stiglitz, *Towards a New Paradigm for Development: Strategies, Policies and Processes*, Geneva: UNCTAD.

6

Panchayati Raj Institutions as the Central Processing Units of Democracy

As already discussed in the previous chapters, development discourse is in vogue. All over the world, the hue and cry over the changing role of the state has attracted the attention of the scholars, academicians, politicians, activists and policy makers equally. The state or the government did not ever wither away rather it has reappeared every time in its changed *avatar* (incarnation). Adam Smith's laissez-faire state to J.M. Keynes' welfare state to neo-liberals' governance state are just some important milestones in the trajectory of changing notion of the state. However, one fact remains at the centre is that state is central to all activities and cannot be ignored at all, especially in the context of globalization.

India, in its initial years of independence, followed with great enthusiasm the Nehruvian model of development (socialist and welfare state model). This centralized model somewhere could not percolate the benefits of development to the grassroots and lacked legitimacy to ensure its sustainability. The whole exercise of CDP or other such centrally sponsored schemes without the real decentralization of powers alienated the poor and marginalized sections of the society from the process of development. Democracy thus needs to be widened and deepened. The government has to work in partnership, and community development should be complemented by experimenting direct democracy (Giddens, 1998).[1]

The country has witnessed the emergence, functioning and effectiveness of the institutions of democratic decentralization in both rural and urban areas. They have withstood the test of time for more than a decade now. Both advocates and critics acknowledge these institutions of local self-governance alike. The representative bodies have expanded the ambit of expectations and raised the participation of people to a new level. Emerging leadership at the grassroots has instilled a new wave of confidence among diverse groups. Marginalized groups are taking keen interest in the process in large numbers, giving a new meaning to local demands and expectations.

The path trodden so far and achievements are indeed encouraging; however, many hurdles remain to be tackled at different levels of policy making and governance. Evaluation of the past experiences reveals specific problems in the functioning, which have been repeatedly expressed in the discussion of governance. The most crucial question at this juncture is: how to build up institutions of local governance as a powerful and effective instrument of democracy in the present context of globalization.

The world is split apart with differences and distortions on the lines of economic and political opportunities. The vehicles of development have to steer the society towards achieving long established goals and objectives. Governance is that steering wheel in the context of globalization. Market orientation cannot free the state of its role in policy making and programme planning. Thus, the state is not disappearing but is getting a makeover done. It is a kind of 'return of government'. A formula called E = RSS depicts a new role of government. Today the government, Etat (i.e. State) is a Responsible, Strategic and Social government (Timsit, 2006).[2]

The idea of development is no more confined to traditional models after the debate opened on new public management. The buzz over sustainable development and inclusive development needs serious attention. Therefore, governments all over the world are reaching out to lowest unit of society and are ready to part with the powers of governance. This aims to invite local participation and set policies in tune with the global forces and changes as well as challenges.

The centralized nation-state is giving way to both supra-national and sub-national institutions. Globalization improves the voice, participation and prosperity of individuals and communities. A few countries like India genuinely sought to use autarchic centralization for the public good and made some modest gains. But most developing countries suffered economic stagnation and political oppression. Self-sufficiency and centralization did not produce prosperous, united countries. Instead they produced more than 100 weak, misgoverned countries which, by the 1990s, needed to be rescued by the IMF. The collapse of the Soviet Union and rise of Deng in China showed that more socialism was not the solution. And, so developing countries began moving in two new directions: globalization and localization (*The Economic Times,* 16 and 23 June 2002).

The academic debate today focuses on developing paradigms to spread the fruits of development to all the sections of society and seek their participation. It is also widely discussed today that development has to be sustainable. Sustainable development is 'development which meets the needs of the present without compromising the ability of future generations to meet their own needs'. Globally, we are not even meeting the needs of the present let alone consider the needs of future generations. The UNDP (1997) defines sustainable human development as 'expanding the choices for all people in society'. This means that men and women, particularly the poor and vulnerable, are at the centre of the development process. It also means the protection of life opportunities for future generations and the natural systems on which life depends. This makes the central purpose of development the creation of an enabling environment in which all can enjoy long, healthy and creative lives.

The Enabling Environment

The ideas of social capital and social audit have today become endearing as these provide ample space for enabling people at the grassroots and give them a chance for their capacity building. However, the social capital available at the grassroots has to be channelized in a judicious manner so as to expand the horizons of development in the way people want it. The public resources under the direct supervision and control of representatives of people at the local level through social audit ensure better delivery of public services and its management is made possible in most economic manner. The impoverished masses, in this way to be elevated and empowered, especially in globalizing world.

The quality and standards set by governance model contributes to achievement of developmental goals, especially in the context of globalization. It aims to achieve inclusive development and also places directives before the government while framing policies and programmes. The fundamental principles of good governance include respect for human rights, political openness, participation, tolerance, administrative and bureaucratic capacity and efficiency. However, when everything happens in the 'public sphere', it cannot take place in isolation. It has to achieve a consensus in the society, and agreement over various issues has to include the voices of especially vulnerable and weaker sections of the society. Good governance then aims to cater to *Bahujan Hitaya Bahujan Sukhay.* This is directed towards achieving an enabling environment where all are participants and recipients of common good. Only a nation's government, civil society and private sector can together facilitate this 'enabling environment', and the challenge is to create a system of governance that promotes these fundamental principles. For this reason, democratic and decentralized governance is increasingly considered a requisite component of development initiatives.

'Globalization should be fair, inclusive and democratically governed. It should provide opportunities and tangible benefits to all people. One of the plausible reasons why decentralization needs to be supported is that companies are accountable only to the shareholders, whereas a democratic institution is accountable to every citizen' (Palanithurai and Ramesh, 2008).

'Decentralization is the direct and faster route to address the issues that globalization brings about. Making proper use of globalization requires access to data and information by the Panchayati Raj Institutions who should be in a position to disseminate to rural community', says S.S. Meenakshisundaram (in Palanithurai and Ramesh, 2009).[3] Integrating institutional reforms in local governance with economic reforms was Gandhiji's far-sighted vision of 'Poorna Swaraj'. Economic reforms and local government empowerment are the two great initiatives launched in the 1990s (ARC, 2006).

It is wrong to equate the 20th century globalization with the 19th century colonialism. In the late 20th century, globalization was not political conquest but economic partnership, creating unprecedented opportunities for the poor to rise. Globalization has brought decolonization, greater flow of capital to developing countries and GDP growth rate of 10 per cent in many developing countries. The fastest growing economies of the world are in Asia, where poverty has also been declining. The world distribution of income shows that the number of people living on 'under-one-dollar-a-day' has fallen from 550 million in 1970 to 350 million in 1999. As a proportion of developing countries population, this is a decline from 17 per cent to 6.7 per cent. Never in the history has poverty fallen so rapidly for so many (*The Economic Times*, 16 and 23 June 2002).

The Challenge

The task ahead is to consider the changing context under globalization and arrange realignment of power and privileges along with matching resources that will enable people to handle their problems in their localized way. The successful examples of local governments around the world and in our own nation inspire us to continue with the process of decentralization. Questioning decentralization or local governance in the pretext of some failed experiments is erroneous. The real question is how to remodel the design fitting the development paradigm, global forces and achievement of MDGs keeping in mind its sustainability as well.

Does decentralization have potential for change? Not at the macro level. But at the (micro) grassroots level, it can empower those who have long been supplicants before statism. Localization can spread the benefits of globalization to the grassroots. Global experience of localization has been very mixed. It works only if rulers are serious about shifting power from the top to the bottom. Creating local governments is not enough: corresponding administrative and fiscal reforms are needed to empower communities with real authority and resources (*The Economic Times*, 16 and 23 June 2002).

Local Governance: Successful Experiments

Following are some of the successful experiments in decentralization and local governance in different parts of the world:

1. Bottom-up approach in north-east Brazil has empowered community and has benefited 2.5 million poor families. It has also helped to reduce the project cost and increase the benefit ratio.

2. In Indonesia, the Kecamatan Development Programme was launched in 1998 to side-step corrupt provincial governments and channel funds directly to villages. It covered 10 million people within three years, and greatly improved outcomes. It is now being extended to another 20–30 million people.

3. The interest of international donor agencies has popularized the concept of 'social funds' as against government funds (which is generally wasted or misused). More than 90 per cent of the World Bank social fund projects have been successful as against 76 per cent of all projects. The Bank is now scaling up social funds into national community-driven programmes in Africa.

4. River-blindness, a disease spread by black flies, once threatened the sight of 34 million people in 11 West African countries. Its eradication has been arguably the biggest development success in Africa. Aerial spraying

by donors was supplemented by community action to distribute medicines, detect and treat the disease. This approach is now being extended to malaria control.

5. In Zimbabwe, centralized management failed to check poaching of wildlife. So, local communities and district councils were made partners in a new programme, called CAMPFIRE. Hunting quotas were sold to hunters, and the revenue shared with communities and local bodies, which now has a stake in checking poaching. Wildlife boomed thereafter.

In South Asia also countries such as Afghanistan, Sri Lanka, Pakistan, Nepal, Bhutan and Bangladesh are actively experimenting with their own forms of decentralization.

In India, experience of decentralization has been mixed. Panchayati Raj is supposed to shift authority and resources to local governments. But most states have sabotaged such a shift. Real local empowerment has been achieved only in a few states such as West Bengal, Madhya Pradesh, Andhra Pradesh, Kerala and Maharashtra.

Local governance has produced major gains in West Bengal. Poverty has fallen and agricultural productivity improved faster than in any other state. But this is a special case of communist-controlled localization, not replicated anywhere else. However, local governments or PRIs cannot function effectively without community participation and civil society partnership. Nongovernmental organizations (NGOs) provide the PRIs necessary wherewithal, that is, knowledge, information, network and resources as well to handle the matters at the grassroots, for example, NGO-PRI partnership successfully prevented the construction of DuPont Plant to make synthetic nylon in Goa.

The phenomenon of rise of local activism, that is, partnership between local government authorities and civil society is one of the ways to design a new developmental paradigm; it is also referred to as 'New Localism'.[4]

PRIs and Community Participation

Spectacular gains have been recorded sometimes through community participation, often unlinked to local governments. Some examples are as follows:

1. In Andhra Pradesh, the irrigation system was silted and run down by the 1990s. Water rates were too low to finance maintenance. Then a new Chief Minister tripled water charges. He made this politically palatable by creating 10,292 elected water users associations to help rehabilitate and manage the irrigation system. In six weeks, the associations completed 22,887 maintenance works at a cost of just $ 28 million. Effective irrigated area increased half a million hectares, and paddy yield rose 10 per cent.

2. In Madhya Pradesh, no teachers wanted to serve in remote tribal areas, where hamlets were often too small to qualify for government schools. Then, a new Chief Minister created an education guarantee scheme. If at least 40 people demanded education, provided a hut for schooling, and chose a local person to be a para-teacher, the government will pay the para-teachers' salary. Within 18 months, 26,000 schools came up with 1.8 million students. Literacy in the state shot up by 20 percentage points in the 1990s. Community participation seems to work better than mere decentralization (*The Economic Times*, 16 and 23 June 2002).

The centrally sponsored schemes such as Sarva Shiksha Abhiyan in the primary education sector, National Rural Health Mission and National Rural Employment Guarantee Act call for greater involvement of PRIs so as to achieve the national goals of development. Seminal contribution of local level bodies actually builds the stepping stone for overall development and empowerment of village community. The dream to cater to rural needs and to fulfil Provision of Urban Amenities in Rural Areas (PURA) is possible if rural local bodies serve as engines of development.

The Kerala Experience

Kerala has set a model for decentralized planning with people's participation and an innovative model for allocating funds to PRIs. In Kerala, the local self-governments belonging to higher tiers do not have any control over the lower tiers. The panchayat presidents are very clear about their role in providing services, and developing plans and implementing them. They take active interest in the proper running of day care centres, primary schools and health sub-centres. They actively look into the maintenance of buildings, regular attendance of the staff and other infrastructure needs. In Kerala, PRIs have initiated the process of participatory natural resource management, watershed management and adult literacy programmes. In some districts, local panchayat authorities also introduced training programmes for capacity building. Participation of women and marginalized community in the development process has lead to their empowerment to a great extent. However, Kerala is not free from elite capture of political power at grassroots level. Over-politicization and interference of local political party leaders often affected the functioning of PRIs making it less objective and more partisan. The People's Plan Campaign (1996) also generated great enthusiasm and demanded people's involvement in the process of local economic development. It was a path-breaking measure as it sought to involve the Gram Sabha in the planning process.

The Karnataka Experiment

The Karnataka state has shown great commitment to the Panchayati Raj legislation. In 1987, it was one of the first states to reorganize its district machinery by transferring the responsibility for district planning to an elected local government structure called the Zilla Panchayat. Here, the emphasis has been on devolution of responsibilities for district planning to locally elected representatives. In Karnataka, since 1987, only one agency called the Zilla Parishad existed that was responsible for both rural development programmes and overall district planning seemingly establishing a more coherent structure.[5] Karnataka is one state which has devolved all the 29 functions mentioned in the 11th Schedule of the Constitution. Thus, it is paving way for greater role of the PRIs.

Reviving, Redefining and Remodelling the PRIs

It is imperative to revive PRIs in the era of globalization and liberalization. Local initiatives and developmental efforts can indeed enhance competitiveness and income generation among the village community. Thus rural–urban divide can be minimized using PRIs as an effective catalyst for making villages assertive, self-reliant and competitive. The revival of PRIs should not undergo another eclipse on the earlier pattern. There has to be genuine commitment to Panchayati Raj as a political value and ideology (Menon, 2007).[6] However, there cannot be any general presumption that decentralization will improve public service delivery or represent the interest of the poor better. Instead, one should expect the outcomes to be context and design specific (Bardhan and Mukherjee, 2007).[7]

Private Sector Participation

In order to redefine the role of the PRIs in the context of globalization, it is very necessary to invite the partnership between the public and private domain. It should become broad and involve the participation of community groups and private groups as well. Local governments are increasingly recognizing that it is clearly in their interest to encourage the development of an energetic private sector and civil society. Local political leaders now perceive that a strong private sector and effective locally based civil society organizations represent, at the least, important allies in their efforts to build institutional and financial resource capacity for their communities. It is for all these reasons that local governments are playing an even more important enabling role in the development of strong private sector and civil society.

Following are various forms of public-private sector-civil society collaboration:

1. Direct government service delivery
2. Contracts and grants
3. Loans and loan guarantees
4. Tax breaks
5. Public regulation of other sectors
6. Publicly established private or nonprofit organizations

Private sector participation can also take a variety of forms, including contracting through competitive biddings, franchise operations (local government acting as a regulatory agency), grants (usually for recreational and cultural activities), vouchers (redeemable by local government with private providers), volunteers (mostly in fire stations and hospitals), community self-help activities (for crime prevention) and private non-profit organizations (for social services). Thus, a mix of delivery systems is appropriate for local public services. In most developing countries, the financial capacities of local governments are quite limited. Fostering private sector participation in the delivery of local public services thus assumes greater significance. Such participation enhances accountability and choice in the local public sector (Shah and Shah, 2006).[8]

Experiences of others also make the path safe to tread, for example,

1. In rural Argentina, NGOs supported by the Inter-American Foundation are collaborating with local governments to establish education and training programmes for low income youth.
2. In El Salvador, private and nonprofit organizations are working with local governments to develop everything from fishing cooperatives to economic development programmes.
3. In Pakistan, community groups have come together to build and operate schools both independently of and in collaboration with local and national governments. In the United States, more government-funded services are delivered through nonprofit organizations (Rosenbaum, 2006).[9]

The 73rd Constitutional Amendment guaranteed the PRIs a legal status and tried to entrench them in the soil so as to strengthen the wide democratic base of India. A one-time assessment of this experiment and evaluation gives inspiring results. However, deep within lies a great concern regarding their sustainable future especially within global changes and challenges. These institutions of self-governance should not merely become agents of state governments. They are to play a role of a central processing unit (CPU) of our democracy. These institutions have the potential to canalize the abundant human resources to handle the local problems in a global way, provided they are given necessary wherewithal and capacity-building exercises. The ambiguity about their role in the governance system, half-hearted compliance by the states of the parent act and superimposed administrative structures at the district, block and village levels are some of issues that need immediate attention.

In the present research, the themes that are explored while studying the PRIs in India in general and in Thane district in particular are social capital, empowerment, participation, social audit, human development and upliftment and good governance. Observations from the field survey lead to one conclusion that the system is at place but its implementation is not as per the letter and spirit of the national and state laws.

It is, therefore, necessary to carve out a structure of governance that ensures maximum participation of maximum people. This can be done only by generating interest and awareness among the village folk. They do not lack enthusiasm, what they lack is the skills to be a part of ıch a process. The government has to play role of enabler and invite their participation. The tremendous amount of social energy that has been released with women coming into political process is unprecedented and this has been the most positive aspect of this whole experience.[10]

The social capital cannot be generated overnight. It takes great efforts on the part of all the organs of the government at state, district and taluka level to organize enabling camps and exercises to train the people in the art of grassroots governance. Mere training also cannot serve the purpose. It is to be followed with providing updated knowledge and information of the latest developments at state, national and global levels. There is a need to rethink and make some value additions to the developmental paradigm modelled on the lines of PRIs.

Recommendations

The whole experience of the participatory governance at the local level is one of the best methods to canalize the abundant human resources we have in India. These resources if tapped in the right fashion can craft wonders. People at the local level are willing to be a part of the decision-making process. What is needed is an autonomous sphere given to them with matching financial capital to decide and design their future. Few suggestions in this regard are as follows:

1. There can be a proposal for a formal tie-up between NGOs and PRIs. It can get legal and constitutional sanction. The NGOs can play a role to get the money from different resources, and Gram Panchayat can help in the implementation of the developmental projects. The problem of financial crunch can be resolved at the grassroots without any aid from centre.

2. Panchayats should try to develop a corpus fund independent of central or state help so as to enjoy the independence of using that money without any control over them.

3. Since panchayats lack taxation powers, a greater autonomy should be given in matters of taxation. The state should be ready to part with state collected taxes and give the panchayats necessary financial autonomy.

4. No governance can be good governance unless it ensures equity and transparency to its people. The RTI Act and the reservation policy are trying to achieve these twin objectives. But, the fact is that a mere declaration of law does not guarantee its proper implementation. It is therefore suggested that there should be an information commissioner in each village appointed from among members of the Gram Panchayat. These commissioners

can be in direct contact with the state chief information commissioner. This will ensure an oversight mechanism well in place and will also enable a social audit of the financial activities of a village.

5. Local institutions have indeed brought hopes and aspirations for the grassroots, especially the marginalized, which of course have to be galvanized through some local initiatives towards development with extensive involvement of civil society.

6. The para-statal institutions mar the whole exercise of local governance. These bodies enjoy a considerable leverage over the elected bodies, which is a matter of concern. The District Planning Committees as envisaged by the 74th Amendment Act under Article 243ZD need to be implemented in letter and spirit. In most states, constitutionally mandated two institutions – District Planning Committee and Metropolitan Planning Committee – either have not been formed or remained defunct where they have been formed. The Planning Commission also issued comprehensive guidelines on 25 August 2006 for the preparation of district plans to be incorporated in the eleventh five-year plan.

7. The rural self-government institutions (the PRIs) need to play a greater role, and for this purpose they have to be further empowered. The long chain of funds transfer to the village panchayats for implementing the development programmes and projects must be shortened. The Gram Panchayat should be made the nodal development agency, instead of the blocks. The empowerment, education (capacity building) and energizing the panchayats will be crucial for the rural development by invoking convergence of the development schemes. For this intent, working for panchayats should be made a career option for the rural

people. Wherever required, in-house technical staff will have to be provided by re-deploying the surplus staffs and oversight arrangements should be in place. The system has to be made transparent, accountable and social audit enabled.[11]

8. The Administrative Reforms Commission, in its report on Ethics in Governance, has strongly recommended the creation of ombudsman in local bodies. This is especially necessary in the context of globalization. It can ensure that injustice and corruption do not get unheard and underdressed.

9. The 12th Finance Commission recommended ₹ 20,000 crore as block grants to panchayats for 2005–2010 (just 4% of the central transfers). The Finance Commission also recommended these transfers to be used for water supply and sanitation. It will be more useful to make such transfers unconditional.

10. In terms of Article 243G, planning is a mandatory function of panchayats. Yet, panchayat-level planning has not been institutionalized in any state other than Kerala. The planning plays a crucial role in the progress of local bodies. We hope that, NITI Ayog will be able to bring in a bottom-up approach to development planning in India.

The picture is clear for the future; the course of action is also in place, the only requirement is to promptly act upon it. The lack of political enthusiasm to cherish PRIs as bodies of local self-governance in the context of globalization may lead to serious ramifications. Javeed Alam, Chairperson of ICSSR, in his keynote address at the national seminar on language, politics and history of Maharashtra referred to the two sets of values taking roots in India. They are participatory values and liberal values. The former are rapidly expanding and the latter are not taking roots in a fast manner.

Alam maintained that the process of decentralization has led to radicalization of democracy and has empowered those who were excluded from the mainstream. The perpetual alienation of underprivileged sections of the society is a challenge before our nation. In the larger landscape of global changes and challenges, these sections are exposed to the market competition as well as technological and information revolution. We have already carved out a new paradigm of development based on participatory democracy through local governance. Yet what remains to be achieved is the expansion of this base to all the states in a uniform manner and it should become a ubiquitous phenomenon. The real stakeholders need to be involved in the policy making and implementing agencies and thus we can aspire to also achieve the MDGs at a desired pace.

As we said earlier, the PRIs are the central processing units of a democracy. They are not merely the elected deliberative bodies or agencies of implementing various developmental schemes. They are the centres that nurture the democratic values and practices and generate consensus in a stratified village community. Today, in the context of globalization, the 'local' has also become a significant contributor to the achievements of set goals. The process of development must start at the roots. Therefore, the PRIs in particular and local governance in general enjoy a prime position. They play the role of a processor to gather information, process it, work on it and achieve the targets for a smaller unit. The successful experiments as discussed earlier testify to one fact that local governance is here to stay and grow in the context of globalization.

Concluding Remarks

The roots of local governance in India could be traced to the Vedic times in the 'Sabhas' and 'Samitis'. As suggested in the *Mantrapushpanjali,* many forms of governance have been experimented in India in the Vedic age, for example, RAJYAM (Police State), BHOJYAM (Welfare State), PARMESHTHYAM (Bureaucratic State), VAIRAJYAM (Self-Rule) (Athavale, 1998). However, these forms of governance did not receive popular attention by the so-called West and that is why we have not got critical acclaim and got buried in the lost past.

This study aimed to search for the changing landscape of local governance especially in the context of globalization. Globalization in India has brought along with it unimaginable and far-reaching changes. These changes have altered the socio-economic fabric of our polity. The market economy, foreign players, advanced technology and information boom have given us myriad opportunities of growth and development. We are now growing at a steady growth rate of 8 per cent. India was one country which could withstand the waves of 2008 recession and still could move ahead on the progress chart. However, the glaring disparities observed across the country testify that development is inequitable. Cities are shining with skyscrapers, yet many parts of them are starving for day's meal. The rural pockets are subjected to 10 to 14 hours of load shedding and giant malls in the cities are illuminated 24 × 7.

Here, few questions remain to be answered, 'Is the growth process all inclusive?' 'Are the non-possessed or disadvantaged getting their due?' and 'How can we enable these people? The anaesthesia of lack of information and deliberate obstructions on the part of political elites has kept them away from the mainstream.

People at the local level, especially in rural areas, are very innovative and enthusiastic. They can create wonders if they are properly guided and empowered. There are plenty of examples across the globe, which pay testimony to the fact that decentralization of powers to local government has given many people an opportunity to be part of shaping their own future. These local bodies, in association with social and citizen groups, have tried to solve many problems at local level, which are results of global changes and challenges.

To get the real picture at the local level, the functioning of few Gram Panchayats from the State of Maharashtra was observed for it stands high in terms of PRI achievements just like Kerala and West Bengal. The Thane district, which also has tribal belts, was picked up for the study. In this district, three talukas, namely, Shahpur, Murbad and Kalyan, were selected. During field work, it was found that people at the rural level, especially women, are very enthusiastic about the whole exercise of the PRIs, although they sometimes lack the vision and direction. They participate in more numbers and resolve their problems using the local machinery.

There is a disillusionment regarding the operational aspects of the PRIs but it can be cured through proper training and capacity building exercise. The abundant human resources can also be converted into social capital with participation of SBOs (society-based organizations), non-governmental organizations and private groups. Thus, the whole idea of local government no more remains a single entity but grows into a broader concept of local governance.

In Shahpur taluka, there is a Gram Panchayat called Gotheghar. This Gram Panchayat, in association with other seven villages, has been successful in getting the World Bank funding for providing water through pipeline to these villages and cure the problem of water scarcity. Another significant contribution of the study is that so far no research on empirical lines of the grassroots institutions in Thane district has been conducted. So, this is an attempt to understand the style and character of institutions in Thane district and to co-relate it with global changes.

People from about 104 villages of Thane district near Mumbai had threatened to break valves of the pipeline supplying water to the metropolis and bring the city's water supply to a halt. The reason is that all their water sources have been completely diverted to Mumbai and they are facing acute drinking water and irrigation crisis. The villages are located in Shahpur taluka, about 100 km from Mumbai. During this uproar, more than 5,000 enraged villagers gheraoed officials of the Municipal Corporation of Greater Mumbai at the Tansa reservoir site and met the District Collector but all in vain. Since 2001, these villagers – mostly tribals and the local Kunbi people – have staged four massive agitations.

The Coca Cola plant, which was to be set up in Kudus village in Wada taluka in 1997, then invited stiff opposition from villagers and the pro-communist All-India Democratic Women's Association because it had reportedly deprived water to thousands of people. 'We do not want the plant to be closed down. We only want proper access to water for villagers and that the company should be charged commercial rates for water', said activist Raju Paranjape. Thus, the examples are testimony to the fact that participation of people along with NGOs lead to greater changes.

The present research has tried to not only project the bright side but also attempted to cherish the achievements rather than cribbing about the pitfalls. However, no claim is made that there are no problems at the PRIs level and is a panacea for all ills.

Notes

1. Giddens, Anthony, *The Third Way: The Renewal of Social Consequences of Modernity*, Cambridge: Polity Press, 1998.

2. Timsit, Gerarrd, 'E = RS^2: The New Return of Government? A Debate on the French Experience', *International Review of Administrative Sciences*, Vol. 72, No. 2, March 2006.
3. Palanithurai, G., and Ramesh, R., *Standpoints on Globalization and Decentralization*, New Delhi; Concept Publishing Company, 2009.
4. Jayal, Niraja Gopal, Pradeep K. Sharma and Amit Prakash (eds), *Local Governance in India: Decentralization and Beyond,* New Delhi: Oxford University Press, 2006.
5. Institutionalizing Decentralized Information Systems for Local Level Planning: Comparing Approaches across Two States in India, *Journal of Global Information Technology Management*, Vol. 3, No. 4, 2000, pp. 45–59.
6. Menon, Sudha, *Grassroot Democracy and Empowerment of People: Evaluation of Panchayati Raj in India*, ICFAI Business School, Ahmedabad 17 June 2007, available at http://mpra.ub.uni-muenchen.de/3839/MPRA Paper No. 3839, posted 07. November 2007/03:29.
7. Bardhan, Pradip and Mukherjee, Dilip. *Decentralization and Local Governments in Developing Countries: Comparative Perspective*, New Delhi: Oxford University Press, 2007.
8. Shah, Anwar and Shah, Sana, *Local Governments in Developing Countries*, Washington, DC: The World Bank, 2006.
9. Allen Rosenbaum, 'Co-operative Service Delivery: The Dynamics of Public Sector-Private Sector-Civil Society Collaboration', *International Review of Administrative Sciences*, Vol. 72, No. 1, March 2006.
10. Vasanthi, Raman, *Globalization, Sustainable Development and Local Self-Government Challenges of the 21st Century: The Indian Experience*, available at http://www.kas.de/upload/kommunalpolitik/Konferenz_09_2000/raman.pdf.
11. Pant, Udaya S., *Empowering the Rural Local Bodies for Faster and Sustainable Rural Development in India,* https://www.researchgate.net/publication/237347917_Empowering_the_Rural_Local_Bodies_for_Faster_and_Sustainable_Rural_Development_in_India.

Appendix

Questionnaire Pertaining to the Delivery of Public Services

1. What are the sources of water used?
2. What is the frequency of the breakdown of the water supply?
3. How good is the quality and quantity of water in the village?
4. What kind of toilets do you use?
5. Were government schemes used to build toilets inside home?
6. What is the condition of the gutters?
7. Do the children go to school?
8. Is there any public health centre facility in the village?
9. Is electricity available in your house?
10. What kind of road is available in the village?

Questionnaire Pertaining to Participation in the Democratic Process

1. Did you vote in the Gram Panchayat election?
2. How regularly do you attend Gram Sabha?
3. Have you raised any issue in the Gram Sabha?
4. According to you how has Gram Panchayat worked?
5. Do you know the name of Gram Sevak?
6. Are you aware of the 73rd Constitutional Amendment Act?
7. Are you aware about the schemes made available to you?
8. What is the quality of understanding about the schemes?

Panchayati Raj

Table 1

Number of Panchayati Raj Institutions (as on 27 February 2007)

States	*Gram Panchayat*	*Inter-mediate Panchayat*	*District Panchayat*	*Total*
Andhra Pradesh	20,538	1,120	23	21,681
Arunachal Pradesh	1,744	152	15	1,911
Assam	2,492	239	23	2,754
Bihar	8,729	533	37	9,299
Chhattisgarh	9,379	146	16	9,541
Goa	189	0	2	191
Gujarat	13,721	224	25	13,970
Haryana	6,177	119	19	6,315
Himachal Pradesh	3,036	75	12	3,123
Jharkhand	4,545	211	22	4,778
Jammu & Kashmir	0	0	0	0
Karnataka	5,654	175	27	5,856
Kerala	991	152	14	1,157
Madhya Pradesh	23,032	313	48	23,393
Maharashtra	28,813	355	35	29,203
Manipur	165	0	4	169
Meghalaya	(a)	(a)	(a)	–
Mizoram	(a)	(a)	(a)	–
Nagaland	(a)	(a)	(a)	–
Orissa	6,234	314	30	6,578
Punjab	12,397	140	17	12,554
Rajasthan	9,328	237	32	9,597
Sikkim	166	0	4	170
Tamil Nadu	12,618	385	29	13,032
Tripura	1,062	40	4	1,106

Cont'd...

...Cont'd

Uttar Pradesh	52,592	820	70	53,482
Uttaranchal	7,237	95	13	7,345
West Bengal	3,354	341	19	3,714
Union Territories				
Andaman and Nicobar Islands	67	9	2	78
Chandigarh	17	1	1	19
Dadar and Nagar Haveli	10	(c)	1	11
Daman and Diu	14	(c)	1	15
NCT Delhi	(b)	(b)	(b)	–
Lakshadweep	10	(c)	1	11
Puducherry	13	6	0	19
All India	2,34,324	6,202	546	2,41,072

Notes: (a) Meghalaya, Mizoram and Nagaland are traditional councils.
(b) Panchayati Raj system is yet to be revived.
(c) Two-tier panchayats: information is not available.

Source: Ministry of Panchayati Raj, Government of India.

Table 2

Number of Elected Representatives in the Three-Tier Panchayati Raj System (as on 1 January 2006)

States	*Number of Elected Representatives*			*Total*
	Gram Panchayat	*Intermediate Panchayat*	*District Panchayat*	
Andhra Pradesh	2,08,291	14,617	1,095	2,24,003
Arunachal Pradesh	6,485	1,615	138	8,013
Assam	23,453	2,148	390	25,991
Bihar	1,17,397	11,611	1,162	1,28,802
Chhattisgarh	1,57,250	2,639	274	1,27,124
Goa	1,439	(c)	33	1,015
Gujarat	1,09,209	2,768	544	86,525

Cont'd...

...Cont'd

Haryana	66,256	2,430	314	57,390
Himachal Pradesh	25,352	1,658	251	20,458
Jharkhand	–	–	–	–
Jammu & Kashmir	–	–	–	–
Karnataka	91,402	2,162	591	56,174
Kerala	16,139	1,009	202	9,669
Madhya Pradesh	3,88,829	4,297	486	2,13,139
Maharashtra	2,23,857	2,877	1,423	1,82,432
Manipur	1,707	(c)	39	1,150
Meghalaya	(a)	(a)	(a)	–
Mizoram	(a)	(a)	(a)	–
Nagaland	(a)	(a)	(a)	–
Orissa	93,781	6,227	854	94,628
Punjab	88,132	1,667	190	50,717
Sikkim	905	(c)	92	965
Tamil Nadu	1,09,308	4,800	483	76,560
Tripura	5,352	193	54	4,037
Uttar Pradesh	7,03,294	33,290	1,338	4,12,146
Uttaranchal	53,988	2,092	226	2,46,192
West Bengal	49,545	6,656	567	46,926
Union Territories				
Andaman and Nicobar Islands	759	42	20	560
Chandigarh	162	15	10	187
Dadar and Nagar Haveli	114	(c)	12	136
Daman and Diu	77	(c)	15	61
NCT Delhi	–	(b)	(b)	–
Lakshadweep	79	(c)	14	63
Puducherry	913	–	–	–

Notes: (a) Meghalaya, Mizoram and Nagaland are traditional councils.
(b) Panchayati Raj system is yet to be revived.
(c) Two-tier panchayats: information is not available.

Source: Ministry of Panchayati Raj, The State of the Panchayats: A Mid-Term Review and Appraisal, November 2006.

Thane District

Thane district forms a part of North Konkan Region, which lies between the Sahyadri hills in the east and the Arabian Sea in the west. It has coastal line of about 113 km. It lies between 18E42' and 20E20' north latitudes and 72E45' to 73E48' east longitudes in the eastern part of Maharashtra. Its east–west spread is maximum at the south, which is about 100 km. The north–south length is approximately 140 km. District headquarter of Thane is about 25 km from the international airport and 35 km from Mumbai city.

Thane is a city in Maharashtra, India, at the head of the Thane creek. It is the administrative headquarters of Thane district. On 16 April 1853, the GIP Railway's first train ever to run in India rolled out from Bori Bunder (now the Chhatrapati Shivaji Terminus) to Thane (sometimes mispronounced as Thana), 34 km away. This marked the dawn of the Railway Age in Asia. Thane covers an area of 147 km and has a population of more than 1.8 million within its municipal limits, according to the 2011 census, making it Mumbai's most populated suburb. Thane is the biggest district in the state with a population 1,10,54,131 and constitutes 9.84 per cent of total population of the state. These figures intensified the debate to split the Thane district into two in order to bridge the social and economic divide between the prosperous south and the neglected rural regions in the north.

It is located to the north-east of Mumbai (it shares that island with the Mumbai City District, with Mumbai Suburban District and with Mira-Bhayandar Municipal Corporation), and partly on the mainland across Thane creek. Spanning an area of about 147 km^2, the city is located at an elevation of 7 meters above sea level. It is surrounded by hills, including Yeoor and Parsik Hills. It is divided politically into two parts by the Thane creek: a stream that courses from the Ulhas River to the Arabian Sea. Two road bridges and one rail bridge connect the two parts of the city. It is one of the oldest cities of India, with its history dating back to about 2,000 years. The city's limits includes Kopri to the south, Wagle estate Naupada, Panch Pakhadi, to the west, Kalwa, Mumbra and Diva to the east and Manpada, Brahmand, Kasarvadavli and Kapurbawdi to the north. On 1 August 2014, the Maharashtra Government announced the formation of the 36th district of Maharashtra, when a new Palghar district was carved out of the old Thane district; it comprised the talukas of Palghar, Vada, Vikramgad, Jawhar, Mokhada, Dahanu, Talasari and Vasai–Virar. Thane is also known as the 'City of Lakes'. The city has around 35 lakes. The most beautiful of them is the Masunda Talao, also known as Talao Pali. The lake offers boating and water scooter facilities. The Upvan Lake is located at the foothills of the Yeoor Hills and is a scenic spot. It is flanked by the Yeoor Hills on one side and the tall Neelkanth Heights on other side, and is a common spot for recreation. The district has triangular shape. Pune and Ahmednagar districts lie on the east. Nashik district lies on the east and north-east, Gujarat and centrally administrated areas of Dadra and Nagar Haveli lie on the north, Arabian Sea forms the north-west boundary, while Mumbai and suburban Mumbai lie on the south. The district is divided into three parts on the basis of its topography. The central portion having Sahyadri ranges and its slope is mainly forest area. The central region covering mostly paddy fields and western part along the West Coast, where horticulture, cultivation of high-quality fodder and vegetables are done. The total geographical area of the district is 9,558 sq. km, which is 3.11 per cent of the total Maharashtra area. The district has 15 tehsils, out of which Shahpur tehsil is the largest area of 1,555 sq. km and Talasari tehsil is the smallest area of 268 sq. km.

Financial Grants Released by the 12th Finance Commission to Villages Under Study of the Present Book

Table 1

Funds Released by the 12th Finance Commission to Ambele Budruk

Year	*First Instalment*	*Second Instalment*	*Third Instalment*
2005–2006	7,180	15,482	
2006–2007	12,422		
2007–2008	7,762	13,066	10,359
2008–2009	11,893	11,833	

Source: Gram Sevak and panchayat records.

Table 2

Funds Released by the 12th Finance Commission to Azade Gao

Year	*Used for*	*Amount*
2009–2010	Yet to be used	₹ 1,88,993
2008–2009	Public health	₹ 1,41,147
(3 instalments)	Insecticides, chemicals and	₹ 1,62,838
	Pipeline	₹ 1,66,993
2005–2006	Gutter works and pipeline	₹ 8,27,506

Source: Gram Sevak and panchayat records.

Table 3

Funds Released by the 12th Finance Commission to Gotheghar

Year	*1st instalment*	*2nd Instalment*	*3rd Instalment*
2006–2007	₹ 54,925	₹ 37,899	₹ 45,430
2007–2008	₹ 28,403	–	–
2008–2009	₹ 47,783	–	–
2009–2010	₹ 37,884	₹ 43,494	₹ 43,275

Source: Gram Sevak and panchayat records.

Table 4

Funds Released by the 12th Finance Commission to Khandpe

Year	*Aid from the Central Government (in Rupees)*
2005–2006	20,124
2006–2007	9,850
2007–2008	6,858
2008–2009	10,359
	8,213
2009–2010	9,429

Source: Gram Sevak and panchayat records.

Table 5

Funds Released by the 12th Finance Commission to Wafe

Year	*Aid from the Central Government (in Rupees)*
2005–2006	31,544
2006–2007	38,137
2007–2008	31,544
2008–2009	19,722
2009–2010	30,199
	30,047

Source: Gram Sevak and panchayat records.

Maps

Map 1

Murbad Taluka

जिल्ह्यातील मुरबाड तालुक्याचे स्थान आणि महत्वाची आकडेवारी

बाब	संख्या
एकुण गावे	२०६
लोकसंख्या	
एकुण	१,७०,२६७
पुरुष	८७,१६३
स्त्रिया	८३,१०४
अनुसूचित जाती	७,४३६
अनुसूचित जमाती	३८,५१८
साक्षरता	
एकुण	६९.१९
पुरुष	८२.६८
स्त्रिया	५४.९७
जमिनीचा वापर (०० हेक्टर)	
भौगोलिक क्षेत्र	९१०
जंगलव्याप्त	२२६
लागवडीखालील	३४७
ओलिताखालील	२३
पिकांखालिल क्षेत्र (०० हेक्टर)	
भात	१६१
नाचणी	-
वरी	३
प्राथमिक शैक्षणिक संख्या	
संस्था	३१६
शिक्षक	८७७
विद्यार्थी	२३,८८२

Map 2

Shahnpur Taluka

जिल्ह्यातील शहापूर तालुक्याचे स्थान आणि महत्वाची आकडेवारी

बाब	संख्या
एकुण गावे	२२८
लोकसंख्या	
एकुण	२,७३,३०४
पुरुष	१,४०,५४७
स्त्रिया	१,३२,७५७
अनुसूचित जाती	११,२११
अनुसूचित जमाती	८९,९९७
साक्षरता	
एकुण	६९.३०
पुरुष	८०.६९
स्त्रिया	५७.१९
जमिनीचा वापर (०० हेक्टर)	
भौगोलिक क्षेत्र	१,५७४
जंगलव्याप्त	७१४
लागवडीखालील	६६४
ओलिताखालील	१५
पिकांखालिल क्षेत्र (०० हेक्टर)	
भात	१४६
नाचणी	३६
वरी	१०
प्राथमिक शैक्षणिक संख्या	
संस्था	४१०
शिक्षक	१,१६५
विद्यार्थी	३३,५६३

Map 3

Kalyan Taluka

जिल्ह्यातील कल्याण तालुक्याचे स्थान आणि महत्वाची आकडेवारी

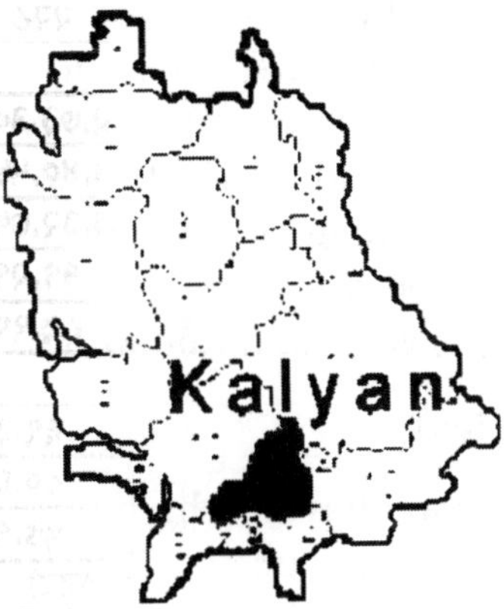

बाब	संख्या
एकुण गावे	६९
लोकसंख्या	
एकुण	१२,७६,६१४
पुरुष	६,७६,७७७
स्त्रिया	५,९९,८३७
अनुसुचित जाती	७४,११६
अनुसूचित जमाती	३४,८९४
साक्षरता	
एकुण	८८.८८
पुरुष	९३.४३
स्त्रिया	८३.७१
जमिनीचा वापर (०० हेक्टर)	
भौगोलिक क्षेत्र	३०८
जंगलव्याप्त	४६
लागवडीखालील	१७७
ओलिताखालील	०
पिकांखालिल क्षेत्र (०० हेक्टर)	
भात	६६
नाचणी	०
वरी	०
प्राथमिक शैक्षणिक संख्या	
संस्था	४१०
शिक्षक	२८४६
विद्यार्थी	१,५०,०२५

Notes from the Field

Thane district was shortlisted for the purpose of conducting ground level research. Three talukas namely Shahpur, Murbad and Kalyan were selected and two villages per taluka were chosen to gather the data from the field. The author using participant – observation method visited all the villages and recorded some important observations which were later thematically arranged and have been discussed in the book. However, the author thought that each and every minute detail of these villages are important windows to understand village level dynamics and hence this section presents the observations of each village individually. The village Panchayats that were visited are – Ambele Budruk, Azade Gao, Gotheghar, Khandape, Wafe and Kalbhunde.

Gram Panchayat: Ambele Budruk

Ambele Budruk is the Gram Panchayat which is quite distant from the Murbad Taluka head quarter. It falls into the interiors of the Murbad Taluka and is approximately 8 km away from Murbad bus depot. Only a few buses from Murbad bus depot during the day are available to reach this village. Otherwise private vehicles or auto rickshaws are used for transport purpose. It was observed that, villages which were not connected pretty well with public transport with the city, in such villages numbers of families owned private vehicles, i.e. either a motor bike or a Tata Sumo. Lack of access to public transport was not a major deterrent factor for many people in the villages visited by the researcher. This could be primarily because village folks are now trying to come out of the obsolete “dependency syndrome”. They do not want to depend on government for every facility. There exists a close link between the changing mindset of people as a result of their contact with the rapidly changing global world.

Ambele Budruk had quite an aware and educated village citizenry. When villagers were questioned, they delightfully said that they are aware of the 73rd Amendment Act. They believe in the benefits of their right to ask questions to the Gram Sevak and Sarpanch or members of the Gram Panchayat regarding the functioning of Gram Panchayat. The common problem in most of the villages was that people are not attending gram sabha meetings in good numbers. Most of the time meetings are adjourned on account of lack of Quorum. The agenda of the meeting is declared well in advance and people are informed also about the meeting. This particular gram panchayat was last elected on 19 November 2007. The total number of members is 7 and all the members are elected unopposed. The post of the Sarpanch is reserved for women.

On the front of availability of basic amenities, this village scores well. This village is 100 per cent electrified. Ambele Budruk however does not have enough water facilities. *Nal Pani Purvatha Yojana* is going on, which is worth ₹ 38 lakh. The Gram Sevak told the researcher that there are two bore well and five wells, 84 individual tap connections and four stand-posts. But villagers responses to the author exposed the ground realities and it was realized that people are not too happy. Irony of this village is that cola bottles and other market beverages were available, but safe and potable drinking water has been a major problem. Under the Bharat Nirman Project, a new water provision scheme is to be implemented where by this village has received a grant of ₹ 13 lakh from the central government. So far, the pipeline construction has been completed for the same and a well and a tank is under construction. This whole project was accepted earlier by the Gram Sabha and people themselves collected 3 per cent of the total money through mass collection for this project. In 2004–05 all the roads were concretized. Yashwant Gram Samriddhhi Yojana is also underway. Gram Sevak pointed out to a very important concern regarding the role of District Rural Development Agency which is an obstacle in the working of Gram Panchayat.

There are a total of eight Malila Bachat Gat in this village. They have been provided with a Big Hall (construction cost was around 8 lakh) to conduct their occupational activities. The village was also given the benefit of Jeevan Sanjivani Yojana whereby 100 per cent concession was given on the interest to be paid on the pending electricity bill, if the village manages to pay at least 50 per cent of the pending Bill amount.

The main occupations are farming and government jobs. Farmers grow cucumber and ladies finger during the summer and sell it to Vashi Market. The main crop round the year is rice. However irrigation facility is not available round the year. This causes a problem for the farmers. The village is 80 per cent literate and many young folks aspire to look for government jobs rather that following traditional agricultural activities.

Gram Panchayat: Azade Gao

Azade Gao is a Gram Panchayat which is quite near to the urban area of Dombivali and has excellent connectivity with the city space. Earlier this area was under the Kalyan-Dombivali Municipal Corporation (KDMC). For 18 years some adjacent village areas boycotted KDMC and wanted to separate away from it. Finally on 12 July 2002, 27 villages got separated; out of which 18 areas were given under jurisdiction of the Kalyan Taluka. These villages now have their own Gram Panchayats. However these areas can also roughly be called little urbanized zones as they are proximate to city areas. Interestingly during the local elections held in Kalyan Dombivali Municipal Corporation in 2015 all these above mentioned areas were again merged within KDMC.

In the 2009 Gram Panchayat Election 8 members of the Gram Panchayat were elected unopposed and for remaining 9 seats elections were conducted. The voting turn out was 60 per cent. The new Sarpanch was a woman as the post was reserved for a woman candidate. Earlier this Panchayat had nine members and three wards. But for 2009 Elections it was increased to 18 members. All members in last election were elected unopposed so there was no formal election. This village was under the influence of political parties like Congress and Shiv Sena.

The village fares excellently on the indicators of availability of basic amenities. This village has five hundread street lights and two dedicated garbage trucks to ensure proper disposal of waste materials. It has one Zilla Parishad School and a number of colleges. There are 40 public toilets in the whole village. The village has won 1st prize in Kalyan Taluka and 3rd prize in Thane district for Saint Gadge Baba Swachhata Abhiyan. The village is also selected for Nirmal Gram Purskar.

This village is one of the richest villages in the Kalyan Taluka and merely 71 people are living below poverty line. This village comes under the jurisdictions of Maharashatra Industrial Development Corporation as well. Most of the village dwellers are educated government servants and hence naturally they are quite aware and also politically active. A pandal has to be set up to organize a Gram Sabha. Participation of people is high. They regularly come to Gram Panchayat with their problems and complaints to keep the members of the Gram Panchayat on their toes. This Gram Panchayat generates good amount of taxes. They used this money for building good roads (Pukka Roads). Mumbai Metropolitan Region Development Authority also had approved 25 lakh for this purpose. They have their own water tank built by their own financial resources.

This village (a rather urbanized zone) seems to be politically active and aware. Residents of the village immediately approach Gram Panchayat office if they come across a problem. This Gram Panchayat received total ₹ 12 lakh as subsidy from the 12th Finance Commission. This money was used for constructions of gutters, water storage tanks, water pipe lines, and public health.

The village also has appointed various committees like Sampoorna Swachhata Abhiyan Committee and Tanta Mukta Committee.

As per the 73rd Amendment Act now Gram Panchayats are also supposed to make registration of births, deaths and marriages at village level. This definitely is a step ahead to bring administration closer to the doorstep of the people. But the opinion of the Sarpanch of this village was that it is burden for us as they earn no income from this. In addition they have to appoint a separate clerk for this function who has to be also paid. To add to the problem if any dispute arises over this matter people come and catch them.

Sarpanch, the Gram Sevak and few members also complained about the role of Mumbai Metropolitan Region Development Authority. As this village comes under urbanized zone the planning and development powers are in the hands of Mumbai Metropolitan Region Development Authority and implementation is through Gram Panchayat. This is a bureaucratic control over the democratically elected body which hampers their power to take decisions for their own development.

The village is equipped with all modern amenities like availability of telephone, cable T.V., DTH service, internet connection, inverters, etc. they are in tune with the changing technology.

This Gram Panchayat has built a water storage tank of 15,000 litres out of the revenue generated from their own resources in order to fulfill the needs in case of scarcity of water. It was the best example of planning and participation of people at the grass roots to resolve their matters in their own way.

Gram Panchayat: Gotheghar

Gotheghar is a gram Panchayat which is located very near to Taluka Shahpur head quarter. This Panchayat has total of eight members which were elected on 26 November 2008 and the voting turn out was 95 per cent. The previous Election was conducted unopposed on 27 November 2003. The total population of the village is 4096 and majority are from Agari Samaj and few are also Katkari.Under the Maharashtra Rural Employment Guarantee Scheme (MREGS) 128 people have registered as labourers and 95 accounts in the village post office have been opened. However, it was commonly observed that, almost in all the villages and people in this district or in these three talukas are not interested in taking advantage of Maharashtra Rural Employment Guarantee Scheme. One of the most important reasons is that the remuneration given as daily wage is hardly ₹ 63 where as they get ₹ 200 per day when they work at private sites. The type of work is also limited.

Land ownership: Very few people have cultivable land or agricultural land of their own. They grow mainly rice, and vegetables especially ladies finger, leafy vegetables and brinjal on their farms. They use the agricultural produce for personal use as well as they sell it in the nearby market. They also sell it at the Krishi Utpann Bazar Samiti, Shahpur.

Occupation: Most of them work as agricultural labourers on land of big farmers. Many women do job of washing and cleaning as domestic servants in the near by city. Some also work in government services or private services.

The researcher visited and attended the Gram Sabha meeting. The agenda of the Gram Sabha was to decide the claims for granting of forest rights under Scheduled Tribes and other traditional forest dwellers (Recognition of Forest Rights) Act, 2005. As per the above mentioned Act Gram Sabha is responsible for determining the nature and extent of forest rights given to the people and prepare a list of beneficiaries (Claimants) and pass a resolution on those claims grating them forest rights. This Gram Sabha meeting was third meeting in a row on this issue. In this meeting all came with their file of official documents and the Sabha was supposed to check its validity and pass it to the next stage. Around 40 people attended this Sabha. To the researcher's surprise the Sabha was attended by more women and three to four of them had formal education. Some of them knew how to read and write. Half of them were illiterate. All present belonged to Scheduled Tribes. One of the women named Tarabai Ramesh Dive who seemed to be a leader of these women, explained the benefits of this Act and had organized them to come to Gram Sabha and avail the benefits of the Act. Very few of them clearly knew for what purpose they had come to the Gram Sabha meeting. The meeting was headed by the Sarpanch. But the female Sarpanch did not say a single word. She was sitting silently and was an inactive participant of the meeting. She left the meeting half way. The meeting was conducted by the Gram Sevak who is appointed by the Panchayat Samiti to help in the functioning of Gram Panchayat. This Gram Sevak was doing his job well explaining the details of the Act. Some of the residents of this village took active interest and participation in the proceedings and were playing a role of self-appointed leaders. Each claimant's file was checked in front of the Sabha and was then approved by the Sabha.

Gram Sevak was of the opinion that Panchayati Raj institutions are benefiting the people and as per 73rd Amendment Act the Gram Sabha was a tool of empowering people, giving them a platform to voice their demands. But many a times the party politics kills the whole idea of democratic governance at the grass root level. Tarabai told the author that she was content with the developmental work done in their village. She said they do regularly attend the Gram Sabha meetings and use this forum to express their opinions. But even they are divided into camps as they belong to one or the other political party. This actually hampers the activities of the Gram Sabha.

World Bank Project of Water Supply: Since 15 October 1993

Gotheghar was one Gram Panchayat which served the purpose this research to gauge a link between global and local. During the discussion with Gram Sevak the researcher came to know that this village in association with other villages has successfully got financial aid from the World Bank to improve the water provision facility. This project jointly serves to the needs of 8 villages namely Gotheghar, Kalambe, Pandit Naka, Rohidas Pada, Konkan Vikas Pada, Ganesh Wadi and Wafe. These 8 villages organised themselves together and sent a proposal to the Zilla Parishad which forwarded the same to the state government. The state government took the help of World Bank and then money was released to these villages. The project is called Maharashtra Pani Purvatha Va Parisar Swachhchta Yojana. This scheme has been in operation since 15 October 1993 and originally ₹ 1,08,20,993 was released. It caters to the need of local villagers and aims to supply at least 17 litres of water per day to per person. For this each day 16 hours of pumping is done to provide approximately 10 lakh litres of water to these villages.

Capacity Building Exercise

On 27 February 2010 at Panchayat Samiti Shahpur, a Mahila Camp for women was conducted to guide the women on legal matters so as to make them legally aware and literate.

Gram Panchayat: Katai

Katai village is very close to a buzzing urbanized area called Dombivali. It is hardly 5 km away from Dombivali. The village was earlier within the purview of Kalyan Dombivali Municipal Corporation and got separated in 2003. The very first Gram Panchayat of the village was elected unopposed. However during November 2009 election 8 members were properly elected and rest 10 were elected unopposed. The voting turnout was surprisingly very good, 100 per cent villagers came out to participate in the electoral process. During the elections and after the election there were some problems between various factions within the village. But on the whole the electoral process had a smooth run. There are total 18 members in this Gram Panchayat. There are two woman members also in the Gram Panchayat of Katai village.

While talking to the members and the Sarpanch on the day of their monthly meeting on 13 January 2010, the researcher found that the male members are deciding the discourse of the meeting. Women members were just nodding their heads. However later it was realized that female members put up their issues indirectly through the Gram Sevika. Sarpanch of the village was reluctant to answer questions asked by the researcher. But they talked a lot over village problems amongst themselves. The agenda of the meeting was to send a request to build a speed breaker on the road outside the village which is supposed to be a highway. Gram Sabha conducted on 8 June 2009 had the agenda to generate awareness for the Sampoorna Swachhta Abhiyan. Importance of using toilets was explained along with how to keep the vicinity clean and hygienic.

In the exclusive Mahila Gram Sabha, all women were told about the importance of water purification. They were also given a bottle of Aquaclore to purify home water. Most of the women from this village attend the Gram Sabha meetings. They come to meetings with their problems and try to solve them. The women of this village are quiet active through Mahila Bachat Gat. They are now aware of various bank activities. They participate in the developmental activities of the village. In this village a novel idea of 'Haldi Kumkum Milan' was executed in which soap boxes were distributed to village ladies as a return gift. The idea behind this was to explain them the importance of washing hands after using toilet (a good measure to take a preventive step against danger of H1N1 Flu).

Sampoorna Gramin Rojgar Yojana, Maharashtra Rural Employment Guarantee Scheme is in operation. Diva Patti, Ghar Patti, Pani Patti, Health tax are various sources of revenue in this village. This is used to pay the salaries and water purification and other developmental activities of the village. This village is also considered as one of the richest villages in the Kalyan Taluka. It has almost all amenities in the village. It is composed of Agari Samaj who are very well-off and prosperous farmers. In the year 2008–09 Katai village received ₹ 57,822 from the 12th Finance Commission. The money was used to buy medicines/pesticides and dustbins. The village has been selected as the winner of Nirmal Gram Purskar 2009.

Gram Panchayat: Khandpe

The journey to reach Kahndpe – a remote village in Murbad Taluka, began from catching a private vehicle on a sharing basis from Kalyan station in Mumbai by paying ₹ 20 to reach Murbad bus depot. It took around 40 to 50 minutes to reach there. From Murbad bus station there are only 3 buses per day going to Khandpe village. It almost took 35 minutes to reach the village. No other transport is available. Few people have their own vehicles. The roads are quite good. On reaching the village and while waiting to meet the Sarpanch, one old lady said out of concern as researcher was searching for the Gram Panchayat office, '*Wait here in my varanda; gram sevika comes on her own two wheeler as she stays in near by village.*' While sitting there researcher quickly initiated a small chat with her. She was questioned about general conditions of the village. Her replies about the functioning of Gram Panchayat were gloomy and pessimistic. The village seemed to be equipped with all modern gadgets like mobiles, T.V., cable connections.

It was observed that the gram sabhas are adjourned due to the non-attendance of village folks. Last gram sabha was conducted on 12 June 2009. The agenda of the meeting was to discuss total sanitation programme and issues related to *Kharif hungam*. But it was adjourned as only 32 people were present. People are not much interested in attending gram sabha. People in this village seem to be little interested in day-to-day political activities. No major political party has any influence here.

Water provision is the best compared to other villages due to availability of khandpe dam nearby. Nal Pani Purvatha Yojana has changed the lives of people here. Apart from this there are four wells, Two bore wells, 10 standpost taps and 74 individual taps available in the village. Under one of the schemes of the centre it was suggested that if people raised at least ₹ 3 lakh through community efforts than state will give ₹ 40 lakh to establish taps in individual houses. This is called Jal Swarajya Yojana.

The state government also offered them to give an aid of ₹ 1 lakh for the construction of public toilets if people raised ₹ 20,000 on their own. It was disappointing to notice that not a single scheme under Bharat Nirman has been implemented in this village. The village has 100 per cent pukka and concretised roads and it was completed through large scale peoples participation. The state government had given an aid of around ₹ 7 lakh to this project. The village is 100 per cent electrified. Many people have been benefited by the Indira Awas Yojana and they have been given aid to build their own house. Under the Rajiv Gandhi Nivara Yojana credit is given to build pukka houses. The Kunabi Marathas are the dominant caste group in the village. Most of them are farmers or are in government jobs. In all the villages which were visited the passion to search for a government job is on rise because of the benefits and security offered by these jobs. The farmers usually grow rice and vegetables like ladies finger, brinjal, chilles and sell it at Vashi market. However there is not a single co-operativge society in this village. They have time again demanded aid for buying seeds and pesticides which they have to buy at double the prices from the regular market.

Under the Maharashtra Rural Employment Guarantee Scheme 650 labourers have registered their names and 150 have been issued a job card. Construction works at three sites have been given permission but it could not begin as labourers do not turn up on account of very low wages offered by the government as compared to what they get by working at a private site.

Paucity of funds is biggest challenge before the Gram Panchayat. It was observed that the village suffered financially also because of low level of tax collection (the estimated demand for 2009–10 was ghar patti – 1,00,210 and pani aptti – 2,22,567 but only 50 per cent could be collected) Peoples' apathetic attitude in the payment of taxes was also a common characteristic feature in the surveyed villages. Other sources of raising funds are not available and this makes them dependent on the centre or state financial aid. The taxes collected are required to be used according to the norms suggested, e.g. 10 per cent of taxes should be utilized for women and child welfare and 15 per cent of it for welfare of SC and ST. Therefore many a times Gram Panchayat is hardly left with any money to use it for any other development purposes.

Researcher attended two Gram Sabha meetings of this village. At both occasions abysmally low attendance was found. The gram sevika said that the agenda of this meeting had no attractive scheme and people were busy in canvassing for the forthcoming Vidhan Sabha Elections (2009). People were busy in the electoral campaigns of Vidhan Sabha Elections during the conduct of Gram Sabha meetings.

There are no incentives from the government, amenities are poor and shabby, agricultural schemes are also not available and financial crunch is their biggest problem. There fore the villagers avoid attending gram sabha meetings. The pukka road towards the village school was built from the Members of Parliament local area development funds. (Bhivandi Lok Sabha Constituency). The state government gave an aid of ₹ 10 lakh to concretize the village roads.

Under Maharashtra Rural Employment Guarantee Scheme, three projects have been approved but have not yet kick started as most of the time the labourers do not come. The reason is low payments compared to private employments. There is only one bore well and other wells are contaminated. For the reconstruction of wells the 12th Finance Commission gave an aid of ₹ 25,000. Gram Sevak said that ₹ 1200 are given for construction of one toilet but it is impossible to construct a toilet with such low financial capital.

Gram Panchayat: Wafe

Wafe is a village in the Shahpur Taluka which is a representative of a developing village. The village is situated 4 km away from the Asangaon station and does not have any facility of public transport. However auto rickshaws and private vehicles are available. The literacy rate is 90 per cent which again reflects the fact that a village nearer to an urban area shows higher rate of education. This village has two Zilla Parishad Schools up to 7th standard and higher secondary school is available at the nearest city. The three Anganwadi cater to the children's education and Sarva Shiksh Abhiyan has catered to the needs of many children. The caste composition of this village reflects that Agari Samaj enjoys a dominant position. The Sarpanch of this village is from Scheduled Tribe. The post of the Sarpanch is reserved for ST candidate.

While taking a stroll of the village and observing things it was noticed that village had almost all the basic amenities and facilities. The roads are concretized and village is 100 per cent electrified. Hygiene is taken seriously in this village and therefore 339 families out of 464 total families have personal toilets. There are total five public toilets in this village.

The women of this village seem to be immensely active and participative. There are 13 Mahila Bachat Gat in this village. A common observation of all the villages which were visited was that women specially are taking a keen interest in the activities of Panchayats and especially are showing great participation through Mahila Bachat Gat. However their political participation in terms of being part of real policy making at the grass root level is still in the process of development. Merely becoming a member of the Gram Panchayat through the reservation policy does not ensure their concrete participation and also does not encourage their political inputs. However their enthusiasm for getting a chance to be a part of this exercise cannot be ignored as well.

Water provision to the households is on continuous basis. The Thane Zilla Parishad Nal Pani Purvatha Yojana is in force and it provides water from the Bhasta river to total three villages namely Gotheghar, Wafe and Kalamba. Each and every household has water supplied through pipeline. The main occupation of the villagers is farming. The main crops are rice and vegetables. They grow ladies finger and other leafy vegetables. They sell their rice at the Shahpur rice mill. Some of them also do fishing for their subsistence living on the Bhatsa and Bharangi rivers near the village.

Indira Awas Yojana and Rajiv Gandhi Nivara Yojana cater to the needs of poor for building their own house. Under Rajiv Gandhi scheme credit upto ₹ 1 lakh is given to the needy persons. The Gram Panchayat prepares a list of beneficiaries depending on the claims made during the Gram Sabha meetings. In this village under the Jawahar Vihir Yojana a farmer can get an aid of up to ₹ 42,000 to build a well in his premises to improve irrigation facility. When the functioning of the Gram Sabha was closely followed it was easy to deduce that this Gram Panchayat is quiet active and participative. The attendance in the Gram Sabha is comparatively good than other villages. The common people approach the Sarpanch and Gram Sevak with their problems and try to get it redressed through innumerable state and central government sponsored schemes. The common complaint expressed by the Gram Sevak and members of the gram panchayat was that for any matter involving financial amount of more than ₹ 5,000 the permission of the junior engineer is to be sought. This creates hurdles in the working of an elected body at the grass roots.

Bibliography

Adhia, Husmuk, Changing the Mindset, *Yojana*, Vol. 49, August 2005.

Ali, Sofi and Rao, Anitha, Reinventing Public Administration for the 21st Century, *Indian Journal of Public Administration*, Vol. 2, April/June 2004.

Amin, Ash (ed.), *Post Federalism: A Reader*, Oxford: Blackwell, 1994, p. 282.

Athavale, Pandurang, *Vyas Vichar*, Mumbai: Sadvichar Darshan Trust, 1999.

Bajpai, Ashok and Verma, M.S., *Panchayati Raj in India: A New Thrust*, Vol. I, New Delhi: Sahitya Prakashan, 1995.

Bandopadhyay, D., Administration, Decentralization and Good Governance, *Economic and Political Weekly*, Vol. XXXI, No. 48, 1996.

Bardhan, P., Bowles, S. and Wallerstein, Michael (eds.), *Globalization and Egalitarian Redistribution*, New Delhi: Oxford University Press, 2006.

Bardhan, Pranab and Mukherjee, Dilip, *Decentralization and Local Governments in Developing Countries: Comparative Perspective*, New Delhi: Oxford University Press, 2007.

Barthwal, C.P., *Good Governance in India*, New Delhi: Deep & Deep Publications, 2003.

Bava, N., Panchayati Raj: An Indian Model of Grassroots Democracy and Decentralized Rural Development, in

Mudacumura, G.M. and Haque, S.M. (eds.), *Handbook of Development Policy Studies*, New York: Marcel Dekker, 2004.

Bennet, R.J., *Decentralization, Local Government and Markets: Towards a Post-Welfare Agenda*, Oxford: Clarendon Press, 1990.

Beteille, Andre, Empowerment, *Economic and Political Weekly*, 34(10/11), 1999, pp. 558–97.

Chahar, S.S. (ed.), *Governance at Grassroot Levels in India*, New Delhi: Kanishka Publishers, 2005.

Chatterjee, Biswajit and Ghosh, Dilip Kumar, Globalization and Decentralized Governance: Reflections on Panchayats in India, *Indian Journal of Public Administration*, Vol. XLIX, No. 2, April-/June 2003.

Chaudhary, Kameshwar (ed.), *Globalization, Governance Reforms and Development in India*, New Delhi: Sage Publications, 2007.

Collins, Paul (ed.), *Applying Public Administration in Development Guideposts to the Future*, Chichester: John Wiley & Sons Ltd., 2000.

Crook, C. Richard and Manor James, *Democracy and Decentralization in South Asia and West Africa: Participation, Accountability and Performance,* Cambridge: The Press Syndicate of University of Cambridge, 1998.

Denters, Bas and Rose, Lawrence E., *Comparing Local Governance: Trends and Development,* London: Palgrave MacMillan, 2005.

Dreze, Jean and Sen, Amartya, *India: Development and Participation*, New Delhi: Oxford University Press, 2002.

Dubey, M.P. and Padalia, Munni (eds.), *Democratic Decentralization and Panchayati Raj Institutions*, New Delhi: Anamika Publishers, 2002.

Dutta, Prabhat, *Decentralization, Participation and Good Governance*, New Delhi: Kalpaz Publication, 2006.

Dwivedi, O.P. and Mishra, D.S., A Good Governance Model for India, *The Indian Journal of Public Administration*, Vol. LI, No. 4, October/December 2004, pp. 719–58.

Ebel, Robert, Logic of Decentralisation and Worldwide Overview, *Talking Points*, 4 September 1998.

George, Fredrickson H. and Smith, Kevin B., *The Public Administration Theory Premier*, Jaipur: Rawat Publications, 2008.

Ghosh, Budhadeb and Kumar, Girish, *State Politics and Panchayats in India*, New Delhi: Manohar, 2003.

Giddens, Anthony, *The Third Way: The Renewal of Social Consequences of Modernity*, Cambridge: Polity Press, 1998.

Godbole, Madhav, *Report of One: Man Committee on Good Governance*, Government of Maharashtra, July 2001.

Goel, S.L. and Rajneesh, Shalini, *Panchayati Raj in India: Theory and Practice*, New Delhi: Deep & Deep Publications, 2003.

Government of India, Report of the Team for the Study of Community Projects and National Extension Service (Chairperson: Balwant Rai Mehta), Committee on Plan Projects, National Development Council, New Delhi, November 1957, Vol. I.

Government of India, Asoka Mehta Committee, *Report of the Committee on Panchayati Raj Institutions*, Ministry of Agriculture and Irrigation, Department of Rural Development, New Delhi, 1978.

Granville, Austin, *Working a Democratic Constitution: The Indian Experience*, New Delhi: Oxford University Press, 1999.

Gupta, D.N., *Decentralization: Need for Reforms*, New Delhi: Concept Publishing House, 2004.

Gupta, Shekhar, The Rurban Mind, *Indian Express*, 31 May 2008.

Halder, Dilip, Democratic Governance is No Panacea: The Experience of India and South Asia, *The Indian Journal of Public Administration*, Vol. L, No. 4, October/December 2004, pp. 1046–69.

Harriss, John, Antinomies of Empowerment: Observations on Civil Society, Politics and Urban Governance, *Economic and Political Weekly*, 42(26), 2007, pp. 2716–24.

Held, David and McGrew, Anthony, *Governing Globalization: Power, Authority and Global Governance*, Oxford: Blackwell, 2003.

Hines, Colin, *Localisation: A Global Manifesto*, London: Earthscan Publications Ltd., 2000.

Holton, Robert J., *Globalization and the Nation-State*, Basingstoke: MacMillan Press (UK), 1998.

Hooja, Rakesh and Parnami, K.K., *Development Administration and Rural Development*, Jaipur: Aalekh Publishers, 2007.

Indian Journal of Public Administration, special issue on 'Good Governance', 1998.

Institutionalizing Decentralized Information Systems for Local Level Planning: Comparing Approaches across Two States in

India, *Journal of Global Information Technology Management*, Vol. 3, No. 4, 2000, pp. 45–59.

Jain, R.B., *Globalization and Good Governance: Pressure for Constructive Reforms*, New Delhi: Deep & Deep Publications, 2005.

Jayal, Niraja Gopal, A Study in Grey, *Indian Express*, April 29, 2008.

Jayal, Niraja Gopal, Sharma, Pradeep K. and Prakash, Amit (eds), *Local Governance in India: Decentralization and Beyond*, New Delhi: Oxford University Press, 2006.

Jha, S.N. and Mathur, P.C., *Decentralization and Local Politics*, New Delhi: Sage Publications.

Kashyap, Anirban, *Panchayti Raj: Views of Founding Fathers and Recommendations of Different Committees*, New Delhi: Lancer Books, 1989.

Kothari, Rajani, Decentralization: The Real Issue, *Seminar*, 360, 1989, pp. 14–19.

Kumar, Girish, *Local Democracy in India: Interpreting Decentralization*, New Delhi: Sage Publications, 2006.

Leftwich, Adrian, *States of Development: On the Primacy of Politics in Development*, Oxford: Blackwell Publishers, 2000.

Lieten, G.K., *Power, Politics and Rural Development: Essays on India*, New Delhi: Manohar, 2003.

Majumdar, A.K. and Singh, Bhawar (eds.), *Historical and Conceptual Development of Panchayati Raj*, New Delhi: Radha Publications, 1997.

Manor, James, *The Political Economy of Democratic Decentralization*, Washington DC: The World Bank, 1999.

Mathew, George, *Panchayati Raj: From Legislation to Movement*, New Delhi: Concept Publishing, 2002.

Mohan, Sudha, *Urban Development and New Localism*, Jaipur: Rawat Publications, 2005.

Mor, Krishna Kumar, *Gram Sabha: Perspectives and Challenges*, Ambala Cantt: The Associated Publishers, 2007.

Mukherji, Nirmal, The Third Stratum, *Economic & Political Weekly*, 28 (18), 1 May 1993.

Munshi, Surendra and Abraham Biju Paul (eds.), *Good Governance, Democratic Societies and Globalization*, New Delhi: Sage Publications, 2004.

Nayyar, Deepak, Globalization: The Past in Our Present, *Third World Economics*, 168, 1997, pp. 7–15.

——, *Governing Globalization: Issues and Institutions*, New York: Oxford University Press, 2002.

Oates, Wallace, *Fiscal Federalism*, New York: Harcourt Brace Jovanovich, 1972.

Osborne, David and Gabler, Ted, *Reinventing Government*, Reading, Mass: Addison Wesley, 1992.

Palan, R., Abbot, J. and Deans P., *State Strategies in the Global Political Economy*, London: Pinter, 1999.

Palanithurai, G. and Ramesh, R., *Globalization: Issues at the Grassroots*, New Delhi: Concept Publishing Company, 2008.

——, *Standpoints on Globalization and Decentralization*, New Delhi: Concept Publishing Company, 2009.

Pierre, John and Guy Peters, B., *Governance, Politics and the State*, Basingstoke: MacMillan, 2000.

Rai, Manoj, *The State of Panchayats: A Participatory Perspective*, New Delhi: Samskriti, 2001.

Rao, Govinda, M. and Singh, Nirvikar, *Political Economy of Federalism in India*, New Delhi: Oxford University Press, 2005.

Rao N. Janardan (ed.), *Globalization: An Introduction*, Hyderabad: ICFAI Press, 2005.

Report of the Administrative Reforms Commission, 2006.

Robertson, Roland, *Globalization: Social Theory and Global Cultures*. London: Sage, 1992.

Rosenbaum, Allen, Co-operative Service Delivery: The Dynamics of Public Sector-Private Sector-Civil Society Collaboration, *International Review of Administrative Sciences*, Vol. 72, No. 1, March 2006.

Sathe, Dhanmajiri, *Does Governance Improve with Globalization? A Case Study of Village Level Institutions in Maharashtra*, India, Institute of Management, Bangalore, 2009.

Schuurman, Frans, J. (ed.), *Globalization and Development Studies: Challenges for the 21st Century*, New Delhi: Vistaar Publications, 2001.

Sen, Amartya, *An Argumentative Indian*, London: Penguin Books, 2005.

——, *Development as Freedom*, New Delhi: Oxford University Press, 2000.

Shah, Anwar and Shah, Sana, *Local Governments in Developing Countries*, Washington DC: The World Bank, 2006.

Singh, Satyajit and Sharma Pradeep, K. (eds.), *Decentralization: Institutions and Politics in Rural India*, New Delhi: Oxford University Press, 2007.

Singh, Surat, *Decentralized Governance in India: Myth and Reality*, New Delhi: Deep & Deep Publications, 2004.

Sivaramakrishnan, *Power to the People: The Politics and Progress of Decentralization*, New Delhi: Konark Publishers, 2000.

Status of Panchayati Raj in the States and Union Territories of India, Institute of Social Sciences, New Delhi: Concept Publishing Co., 2000.

Stiglitz, Joseph, *Globalization and its Discontents*, London: Penguin Books, 2002.

——, *Towards a New Paradigm for Development: Strategies, Policies and Processes: Lectures*, Geneva: UNCTAD, 1998.

——, *Economics of the Public Sector*, New York and London: W.W. Norton & Co., 2000.

The World Bank, *Governance and Development*, Washington, DC: The World Bank, 1992.

The World Bank, *Overview of Rural Decentralization in India*, Vol. III, 2000.

Thomas Issac, T.M. and Franke, Richard, *Local Democracy and Development: People's Campaign for Decentralized Planning in Kerala*, New Delhi: Leftword Books, 2000.

Timsit, Gerarrd, $E = RS^2$: The New Return of Government? A Debate on the French Experience, *International Review of Administrative Sciences*, Vol. 72, No. 2, March 2006.

Tremblay, Reeta C., Globalization and Indian Federalism, *IJPA*, Vol. XLVII, No. 2, April/June 2001.

United Nations Development Programme, *A Global Analysis of UNDP Support to Decentralization and Local Governance Programme 2001*, September 2002.

——, *Decentralization in India: Challenges and Opportunities*, New Delhi: Human Development Resource Centre, 2000.

——, *Overview of Decentralization World Wide: A Stepping Stone to Improved Governance and Human Development*, 2nd International Conference on Decentralization, July 2002.

Valmiki Ramayan, Sadvichar Darshan Trust, 1998 Sanskriti Chintan, Sadvichar Darshan Trust, Mumbai, 1998.

Vittal, N., Governance for Development, *The Indian Journal of Public Administration*, Vol. L, No. 1, January/March 2004, pp. 30–8

World Commission on Social Dimension of Globalization, *A Fair Globalization: Creating Opportunities for All*, New Delhi: Academic Foundation, 2006.

Internet Sources

Bharat Nirman and Flagship Programmes 11th Five Year Plan, available at http://www.planningcommission.nic.in/plans/planrel/fiveyr/11th/11_v3/11v3_ch6.pdf.

Bharat Nirman: A Time-Bound Plan for Rural Infrastructure, available at http://zprajnandgaon.gov.in/technical%20documents/Bharat%20Nirman.pdf.

Crook, Richard, and Sverrisson D.S., *Decentralization and Poverty Alleviation in Developing Countries*, IDS Working Paper 130 (Brighton: DFID), available at http://www.ids.ac.uk/files/dmfile/wp130.pdf, 1999.

Decentralization & Panchayati Raj Institutions (PRIs), available at http://planningcommission.gov.in/plans/mta/mta--9702/mta-ch10.pdf.

Decentralization in India: Challenges and Opportunities, available at http://www.in.undp.org/content/dam/india/docs/decentralisation_india_challenges_opportunities.pdf.

Does Governance Improve with Globalization? A Case Study of Village Level Institutions in Maharashtra, India, available at http://www.igidr.ac.in/pdf/publication/PP-062-17.pdf.

Economic Survey of India, available at http://indiabudget.nic.in/es2007-08/esmain.htm.

Eleventh Five Year Plan Chapter on Governance, available at http://www.planningcommission.nic.in/plans/planrel/fiveyr/11th/11_v1/11v1_ch10.pdf.

Eleventh Five Year Plan Chapter on Inclusive Growth, available at http://www.planningcommission.nic.in/plans/planrel/fiveyr/11th/11_v1/11v1_ch1.pdf.

Fifteenth Anniversary Charter on Panchayati Raj: Inclusive Growth through Inclusive Governance April 2008, available at http://www.panchayat.gov.in/documents/401/84079/FinalCharter-English.pdf.

Garrett, Geoffrey, Globalization and Decentralization, available at http://leitner.yale.edu/sites/default/files/files/resources/docs/2000-03.pdf.

Globalization, Sustainable Development and Local Self-Government Challenges of the 21st Century: The Indian Experience, available at http://www.kas.de/upload/kommunalpolitik/Konferenz_09_2000/raman.pdf.

Godbole, Madhav, Report of the One Man Committee on Good Governance, July 2001, available at http://maharashtra civilservice.org/cms/downloads/516b0f962943f.pdf.

Human Development Report, Deepening Democracy in a Fragmented World, UNDP, available at http://hdr.undp.org/sites/default /files/reports/263/hdr_2002_en_complete.pdf, 2002.

Human Development Report: Maharashtra, UNDP, http://www.in.undp.org/content/india/en/home/library/hdr/human-development-reports/State_Human_Development_Reports/ Maharashtra.html, 2002.

Jayader, A., Note on Good Governance, IMG Kerala, available at http://www.img.kerala. gov.in/docs/downloads/gg.pdf.

Jha, Shikha, Panchayats: Functions, Responsibilities and Resources, available at http://fincomindia.nic.in/writereaddata/ html_en_files/oldcommission_html/predocs/speech/shikha%20jha.pdf.

Manor, James, Local Governance, available at http://www.gsdrc. org/docs/open /PO40.pdf.

Menon, Sudha Venu, Grassroot Democracy and Empowerment of People: Evaluation of Panchayati Raj in India, ICFAI Business School, Ahmedabad, 17 June 2007, available at https://mpra. ub.uni-muenchen.de/3839/1/MPRA_paper_3839.pdf.

Overview of Decentralization Worldwide: A Stepping Stone to Improved Governance and Human Development, available at http://www.cities-localgovernments.org/committees/dal/Upload/ library/overviewofdecentralisationworldwide_work_2002.pdf.

Parker, A. and Serrano, R., Promoting Good Governance through Social Funds and Decentralization, September 2000, available at http://www1.worldbank.org/publicsector/decentralization/ Social%20Funds.pdf.

Parker, A. and Serrano, R., Promoting Good Local Governance through Social Funds and Decentralization, available at http://www1.worldbank.org/publicsector/decentralization/Social%20Funds.pdf.

Report of the Task Force on Panchayati Raj Institutions (PRIs), available at http://planningcommission.gov.in/aboutus/taskforce/tsk_pri.pdf.

Report of Working Group on Report of the Working Group on Democratic Decentralization and Panchayati Raj Institutions, available at http://planningcommission.nic.in/aboutus/committee/wrkgrp11/wg11_demo.pdf.

Sahni, S., Engaging with Participatory Local Governance in India, available at http://unpan1.un.org/intradoc/groups/public/documents/un/unpan013176.pdf.

Simpson, Rachelle, A Comparative Study of the Impact of Globalization on the Development of Bangladesh and Tanzania Victoria University, available at http://vuir.vu.edu.au/1451/1/simpson.pdf, 2007.

Singh, B.P., The Challenges of Good Governance in India: Need for Innovative Approach, available at http://www. innovations. harvard.edu/cache/documents/1034/103461.pdf.

The Bombay Village Panchayat Act, 1958, available at http://www.panchayat.gov.in/documents/10198/350801/Bombay%20Village%20Panchayat%20Act%201958.pdf

The Maharashtra Zilla Parishad and Panchayat Samiti Act, 1961, available at http://www.panchayat.gov.in/documents/10198/350801/Maharashtra%20Panchayat%20Act%201961.pdf

Twelfth Finance Commission Report, available at http://fincomindia.nic.in/writereaddata/html_en_files/oldcommission_html/fcreport/Report_of_12th_Finance_Commission/12fcreng.pdf.

Yusuf, Shahid, The Changing Development Landscape, available at https://www.imf.org/external/pubs/ft/fandd/1999/12/pdf/yusuf.pdf.

Index